THE ENCYCLOPEDIA OF WEALTH BUILDING FINANCIAL OPPORTUNITIES

MONEY MANUAL NO. 1—PLANT YOUR DOLLARS IN REAL ESTATE AND WATCH THEM GROW
The Basics Of Real Estate Investing

MONEY MANUAL NO. 2—INVESTMENT OPPORTUNITIES OF THE 1980'S
Wealth Building Strategies In The Stock Market, Gold, Silver, Diamonds...

MONEY MANUAL NO. 3—SECRETS OF THE MILLIONAIRES
How The Rich Made It Big

MONEY MANUAL NO. 4—DYNAMICS OF PERSONAL MONEY MANAGEMENT
How To Save, Manage, And Multiply Your Money

MONEY MANUAL NO. 5—THE NEW AGE OF BANKING
Secrets Of Banking And Borrowing

MONEY MANUAL NO. 6—HOW TO START MAKING MONEY IN A BUSINESS OF YOUR OWN
A Guide To Money Making Opportunities

MONEY MANUAL NO. 7—HOW TO SAVE ON TAXES AND TAKE ALL THE DEDUCTIONS YOU ARE ENTITLED TO

Plant Your Dollars In Real Estate And Watch Them Grow

The Basics of Real Estate Investing

Published By

George Sterne
Profit Ideas
8361 Vickers St., Suite 304
San Diego, CA 92111

ACKNOWLEDGEMENTS

The publishers wish to express thanks to Gene Edelbrock & Russ von Hoelscher for their contribution of research and writing to this book.

PLANT YOUR DOLLARS IN REAL ESTATE AND WATCH THEM GROW

The Basics of Real Estate Investing

Table of Contents

Preface

FOREWORD

If you could start a garden and knew how to grow a giant money tree by following step-by-step planting instruction, wouldn't you get busy planting your huge "tree of wealth"? Of course you would. You would learn to fertilize properly, giving enough but not too much. You would learn how to carefully prune your budding new tree to assure maximum growth and yield. You would give the best tender loving care to your young tree to help it mature into full blown maturity, heavy-laden with "large green" leaves.

The very same principles apply to the growing and cultivation of a vast real estate empire. You can become wealthy beyond your wildest dreams by selective, systematic investing in real estate. More people have become millionaires through real property investments than all other forms of investments combined.

Let this manual give you the right guidelines that can point you towards huge success.

This manual has been completely revised and includes many new workable, smart investing tactics and techniques. Of special interest in these days of high interest rates is an informative new chapter on creative financing.

This manual can serve as the future soil in which you can grow your own money tree. Plant your seed now.

Chapter One

THE CASE FOR REAL ESTATE

"... Every person who invests in well-selected real estate in a growing section of a prosperous community adopts the surest and safest method of becoming independent, for real estate is the basis of wealth ..."

Theodore Roosevelt

"Buying real estate is not only the best way, the quickest way, and the safest way, but the only way to become wealthy ..."

Marshall Field

"... Ninety percent of all millionaires become so through owning real estate. More money has been made in real estate than in all industrial investments combined. The wise young man or wage earner of today invests his money in real estate ..."

Andrew Carnegie

In studies of the ultra wealthy it has become evident that they didn't earn all that money — few have. The wealth has come from investing money. Almost all the new millionaires, and there are many, have done it by investing it and sheltering it in real estate. Their money works for them and grows.

The ominous inflation we have been seeing has been eroding our buying power. The average wage earner is finding that he can't buy as much as he used to and that his budget keeps getting tighter and tighter. He is having trouble just maintaining his usual life style, much less save anything. How then can we become millionaires? We could invest in the stock market. However, over the past decade, the stock market has not kept pace with real estate as an inflation-beating investment. Real estate has consistently risen in value nationwide, while the market has had many peaks and valleys.

Tax sheltered annuities and savings programs like IRA and Keogh are good. They definitely build up and you get a good tax advantage from them. The finer programs are generally offered by the better insurance companies. Life insurance is also a good way of saving. Why can these companies offer their subscribers a 2.5%–3% compounding on their deposits? Simple answer — BECAUSE THEY INVEST IN REAL ESTATE. Who are the richest corporations around? The insurance companies, because they own so much land! How do they do it? They use Other People's Money — (their policy holders) to buy land.

How good an investment is putting money in a bank or savings and loan? If you are living in a state of inflation of at least 6% and they are paying you less than that in interest, you are already losing money. The interest they pay you is also taxable, so you are losing more than you think. What are they doing with your money anyway? You guessed it. As much as their government charter will allow, they are sinking it into real estate. There obviously is a better way to invest than leaving our money in a bank or savings and loan.

What makes income property such a good investment?

There are several advantages that real estate offers that other forms of investment can't offer:

1. It is a hedge against inflation—as things become more costly, so does your property — many times it is faster than the inflation itself;

2. You get a tax write-off and pay less income tax even though you may take in more money than you are spending on your property;

3. You can finance most of your wealth with **Other People's Money**;

4. The property, if structured properly, pays for itself as it goes along;

5. Your tenants, by making your principle payments, are actually financing your wealth.

Then, if millionaires make it in real estate, and savings and loan companies make in real estate why should we not invest with them? Why don't **we** invest in real estate?

Chapter Two

THE REAL ESTATE MARKET —
IT'S HERE TO STAY

Can you picture taxes going down? How soon do you expect the cost of labor to go down? You probably have the same feeling for building costs. The whole world is in an upward inflationary spiral. The government is paying previous debts with inflated dollars. The government cannot let go of the tiger's tail. We are all paving the way with inflated money. There are few things that can act as a hedge against inflation. Some of these things can even make money for you as you go along. Regardless of what they are, they cannot do for you what real estate can do. Real estate can be bought without risk, with leverage, used as collateral, doesn't take an educated eye (as would gems and antiques), cannot be stolen, can be financed, traded, can be rented so that it pays its own way and reduce the amount of income taxes you pay.

By the law of supply and demand, real estate has to be worth more in the future than it is now. There is **not** unlimited land. Many cities have already reached their saturation point in water and sewer supply, in addition to overtaxed electric and gas supply. We have already foreseen that the costs will only make the cost of building new projects go up. This automatically makes the existing property values rise.

Right now you could throw a dart at a map of the United States and make money buying the property you hit — some better than others, but it all rises commensurately.

There are many areas that are sure bets, but we are calculating in truth, reality and real estate.

Another reality is that the country (the world) has been in an inflation rate of at least 10% for years, whereas the rate of appreciation of real estate has been consistently substantially higher than that rate. In Southern California the rate of inflation (or appreciation) the last few years has been close to double that of the national inflation rate. Can you see why this makes such a wonderful hedge for your invested dollar?

NOTES

Section II

HOW TO PLANT YOUR
REAL ESTATE TREE

Most gardens are judged by their beauty. Is a grove? No, it is judged by how much it produces. Would you suffer to have an ugly, stinky, noisy oil well in your backyard? (Undoubtedly you wouldn't have to suffer with it for long.) Let's develop the perspective that it's not our property, it's our bank statement.

Chapter Three

CAN'T TELL YOUR GARDEN WITHOUT A PLACARD

To make your money tree grow, study your gardening basics. In order to safeguard your plant you need to understand concepts of irrigation, soil content, fertilizer and sun intensity. Similarly, you need to understand a few concepts about real estate investment.

What Makes it Grow? — Appreciation

The real money in real estate investing is made in appreciation. Accurately projecting the increase in property values is difficult since the increase depends on inflation, investor demand and supply of available property. However, appreciation and inflation go hand in hand. Real property always goes up in value with inflation.

There is no profit in keeping your money in a savings account because inflation and taxes render your investment useless. Of course, the bank percentage is guaranteed and is paid without management hassle: you know that your money will be there at the end of the year and that you don't have to lift a finger to earn the interest. To get the returns that real estate can earn, you must take the risk that real estate investment requires; you must cope with management problems; you must learn that your financial independence comes at a price, but the price is worth it. Nothing worth anything is free. So, you must anticipate inflation and appreciating values.

For years we have been living in a sustained period of inflation (at least 6%). For example, if you take a home of $50,000 appreciating (inflating) at 6% it would be

$$\$50,000 \times .06 = \$3,000$$

After one year, the property would be worth

$$\$50,000 + \$3,000 = \$53,000$$

Appreciation through inflation is a key factor in what we're proposing.

To cite an example of another form of appreciation, let's look at a family with 4 kids and 4 dogs buying a home at the end of the street. Shortly after they are in, the street is continued, bringing in a shopping center several blocks down, and then continuing on giving freeway access.

The property automatically becomes more desireable (appreciation) even though the kids are detrimental to the house, and the dogs are wrecking the yard (depreciation).

How Much Fertilizer? — Leverage

Leverage makes real estate advantageous. Think of using a small lever to move a large boulder. Although you could never move the boulder by yourself, with a lever it is easy. In real estate, leverage is controlling many investment dollars with only a small amount of money. In other words, when we operate on credit — that is, on other people's money — we use "leverage." Leverage is the big basic principle behind all successful real estate buying.

Smart investors use borrowed money in most realty investments even when they can buy the property free and clear. They keep their own cash outlay to a minimum. They will pay high interest on borrowed money if their overall return will be higher yet. The more leverage they can use (i.e. only a small amount of their own money with the greater part being other people's money) the bigger is the potential for a high rate of return on their money.

Whenever you find a way either to borrow at less cost or to increase the percentage of borrowed money you use in a real estate transaction, you enhance the potential benefits of leverage. The less of your own money used in a transaction, the higher your potential rate of return. You can get more "leverage" by:

— borrowing at a lower interest

— taking out a bigger mortgage in proportion to your down payment

— making a smaller down payment

There are some disadvantages to leveraging. For example, when an owner has a thin equity, he can be in real trouble when the economy takes a downturn. Poor property management must also be watched for, as it can eliminate an owner with a thin equity. Leverage also can attract the shoestring operator who tries to build or purchase beyond his means through leveraging. Leverage, to produce lasting results, must be used wisely. When properly used, leverage is a very useful tool. Real estate is one of the few areas where an average investor with average knowledge can borrow other people's money to use leverage in investing and, by doing so, can increase his own return.

Our plan is predicated upon the concept that the more property you control in your name, the more appreciation you will have. For illustrative purpose let's take 3 sets of investors with $50,000 to invest. We will assume an inflation rate of 6%.

The **1st Investor** plunks all his $50,000 in a house and owes nothing (100%).

The **2nd Investor** puts his $50,000 down and owes $50,000 against a $100,000 house (50% equity).

The **3rd Investor** wrangles a deal to put his $50,000 against some apartments worth $500,000 (10% equity).

Investor #1	Investor #2	Investor #3
50,000 home	100,000 home	500,000 apartments
3,000 6% appreciation	6,000 6% appreciation	30,000 6% appreciation
53,000 value in 1 year	106,000 value in 1 year	530,000 value in 1 year
3,000 divided by 50,000	6,000 divided by 50,000	30,000 divided by 50,000
is	is	is
6% gain on 50,000	12% gain on 50,000	60% gain in 1 year
investment in 1 year	investment in 1 year	

Are the Roots Down There? — Equity

Equity build-up results as mortgage payments gradually reduce the loan — it is a return on invested dollars. Equity build-up is important. The bigger your equity in the property, the wealthier you are on paper; that is, equity build-up represents a financial benefit. It's easy to create real estate equities if you have imagination; unfortunately, it's easy to lose them if you don't. Here's a brief example:

If you own a $50,000 home, and you owe $40,000 against it, your equity is $10,000.

$$\$50,000 - \$40,000 = \$10,000$$

As payments are made and monthly deposits are paid toward the principle, your equity increases. Also, as demonstrated above, as the property appreciates your equity increases. This is one of the main objectives of our investment program. It is also axiomatic that the more property you hold (by using leverage) the more your equity grows through appreciation or inflation.

Does It Need Much Water? — Depreciation

As long as we're in this rental business, the government gives us a good assist. They know our buildings won't last and that eventually we'll have to replace them. They will permit us to defray that depreciation over a number of years. We can deduct this as an expense to the business. If we have a $50,000 building on a $20,000 lot, we can charge off that $50,000. (The $20,000 on land theoretically never wears out.) If we were to elect to charge off this $50,000 evenly over 25 years*, we could include $2,000 annual expense to **depreciation**. This is what makes income property so lucrative.

There are generally four types of income-producing property. These depend on the property's use:

(1) real property held for sale to customers

(2) real property held for the use in trade or business

(3) real property held for investment purposes only

(4) real property held for the production of income (generally through residential rentals)

So, as you can see, the last classification is the only one that is actually "income" producing; the other ones produce income through appreciation or "forced inflation". Forced inflation results when you inflate the value of the property by improving it, thus making it more desirable.

If the property you hold is for sale to customers (1), the IRS considers you a dealer in property, thus you cannot take depreciation. The property is treated like inventory or a business product; the gain is ordinary income, and the loss is ordinary loss.

Real property held for use in a trade or business (2) — e.g. a restaurant or a pool hall — is another matter. If you sell such property at a loss, you have a loss carry-back or forward that can be "subtracted" from your ordinary income. You can carry it back for the previous three years (and get a tax refund) or forward for the next five years (and have lower taxes). You are allowed to depreciate such property and also deduct your ordinary business expenses.

Real property held for investment (3) is usually not depreciable because it doesn't have improvements on it. If you hold this type of property longer than twelve months, you can take capital gains and losses. You can also deduct management costs, taxes and maintenance costs, in addition to interest payments on loans against the property. You might also be able to take a deduction for depreciation if the property produced income.

Real property held for the production of income (4) is the category of property we are primarily interested in. For this kind of property, you are always allowed to take depreciation allowances. Usually, such property is commercial, nonresidential, industrial or residential property, such as apartments, which are rented. Although the apartments may be bringing in more money than we are spending, through the inclusion of depreciation, **on paper** it looks as if we are losing money. This loss on rental property can be subtracted from our earned income (salaries, etc.) We pay less tax because we netted less. This is called our **tax shelter**. At this point, let it suffice that we may not want to lean too heavily on depreciation at the beginning of our program. The government aims to get it back sooner or later.

Can We Graft on Another Producing
Branch? "New Starter"

After you get your tree bearing, you may be able to improve your yield by grafting on another bloomer. Your main plant could be embellished upon by including with it a new plant or piece of property. Anytime you can pick up a bargain, you could include it with your main package when selling or trading to increase your equity and depreciation. This

25

will also shorten the time interval needed between your main property transactions.

Now we have the basics for our garden. Through keeping our **equity** low, we use **leverage** for **appreciation and depreciation**. We will service our tree around these concepts. If we have a 10% equity, 90% of our crop is done with **Other People's Money** — welcome to the **OPM** Club. If forces other than your own capital can make you money, why not join their team — or better yet, have them join your team.

*There are several popular forms of depreciation for different purposes. The most basic illustrated above is called **Straight line.**

See Appendix E for different kinds of depreciation. Appendix F for their application.

NOTES

Section III

How to Plant Your Money Producer
for Sturdy Growth

Monopoly

Most of us at one time or another have played the game "Monopoly". There are some valuable lessons to be learned even though it is only a game — the person with no property is at the mercy of those who have it. The rich get richer, the poor get poorer.

In the game, it is a matter of chance as to who gets the right properties first. In real life we need not wait — we should determine our course of action and then do it.

Chapter Four

LET'S START DIGGING!

Do you have life insurance? If you have a whole life policy (not term), you have paid in some cash that has been accruing interest. (The insurance company has been investing in real estate, remember?). They will be glad to lend you these cash values. Sounds great? The best is yet to come. The rate at which they lend this is between 4% and 6%! There are few bargains like this around anywhere. Certainly you are going to make more than 6% on your real estate investment. (Remember the chart on page 7 of three investors?)

So you don't have an insurance policy. How about your dad or father-in-law? They would have much more in it available to borrow. If you borrowed say $10,000 of his money, you could offer him a 2nd trust deed held on your new investment and pay him back with higher interest. His insurance money is secured, he is making more on it than if it stayed in his account, and you are on your way.

If you have an equity in your home, you can start here. Go to your lender and ask him to increase your loan to the maximum. It will raise your payments, and interest rate, but it will be worth it when you put it to work ...

If you can build up an equity in income property to three times the amount of the value of that home you have, you probably wouldn't be satisfied with that house any longer anyway.

Income property is such a good deal that many people are buying new homes for 10%–15% down and then renting them out. In anticipation of the great appreciation they will get, they think nothing of renting these houses for several hundred dollars less than the payments (an example of *negative cash flow*).

Would you not be better off to sell your house to invest in real estate, and then rent one of these new homes yourself?

You don't own your home? How about your dad, father-in-law? Again, offer him the security of that *second trust deed* — he will probably be glad to help you. You **could** offer him a partnership and buy him out later (although I'd prefer other routes first).

Are you a veteran? There are some fabulous opportunites for vets to buy with little down. If you can capitalize on this, it will get you started. You can trade this house later on.

Do you own your car? Is it worth a year or two driving a cheaper car to send you on the road to success? Remember our dedication to the money tree? If you have an equity in a good car, sell it and drive a less expensive model for a short time.

In the next chapter we will show you that the more money you can start with, the better off you are. How about using several of these above sources of money — it will all come back soon, greatly multiplied.

If you have no credit anywhere, there are still ways to get into real estate.

In some cases a seller will be interested in leasing the property to you and giving you the option of buying it at or before the end of the term *(lease option)*. A contract of this type can be flexible as you two want to make it. Many times the lease rent is applied as a down payment, but not necessarily. It is a good way for the intended buyer to take a piece of property off the market for a year or so. If the property appreciates higher than anticipated, the person leasing has made some money. Ordinarily, to compensate the seller for this risk, the price is jacked up. Again, it is a contract written by two people. How good a bargainer are you?

A statement should certainly be included in the lease giving you the right at any time to sell your option or the property. If you don't sell you must eventually qualify to assume the existing loan or create a new one.

For someone who has no present money or good credit, he can still tie up a piece of property and enjoy the benefits of it. This vehicle has several names, but is primarily known as the land contract. The potential seller keeps title in his name and the buyer makes payments as contracted. Everything is OK as long the buyer keeps honoring his contract. If he defaults, he is not offered the protection of a default in trust deeds. However, the payments are still being made in the name of the seller. The lending institution does not have the right to refuse such a transaction.

This situation can linger on until the buyer can get OK'd by the lender — or until he has a good sized equity in property and/or he can get it refinanced elsewhere, or sold.

Warning — if the seller is unethical, he can sometimes take

31

advantage of you — title transfer cannot always be assured. This route should bear the scrutiny of your attorney.

If we still haven't succeeded in getting you into your first property, let's try another way. Ghetto property is always turning over and you can get into it more cheaply than other property. If you haven't been able to get started with any of the aforementioned methods, you need help. Swallow a little pride and buckle up for a year. I'll bet there are VA or FHA *foreclosures* down in the ghetto or fringe area that you can get into for a song. — It would oblige you to live there for a short time (at least legally), but then you're free to sell or exchange. In chapter 8 there are some suggestions on how to pick up some of this property for little or nothing — you're at the point where you have little to lose except the difficult position you're in.

There is still another way if you can afford to invest a certain amount of cash per month. You would need to join hands with several others in a group investment. To do this you would need to find a real estate syndicator who specialized in group investment. An imaginative syndicator can be a magician if you can find him.

It is not so important which technique or approach you use. What is important is that you do something and get underway and with as much equity as you can possibly conjure up. All of the ways are good — but it is important to get started under intelligent and well thought out guide-lines.

NOTES

Chapter Five

BUY IT RIGHT!

The three most important elements to consider when buying property are location, condition and financing. The four kinds of return from a normal income property investment are:

1. Cash flow — money left over after all expenses and mortgage payments have been made.

2. Equity buildup — results when mortgage payments gradually reduce the loan.

3. Tax savings — come from tax advantages of real estate ownership.

4. Appreciation — occurs as the property increases in value.

By being alert and sensitive to trends, you will know when to buy, when to sell, when to build and when to hold on to your investments. Facts on neighborhood trends, the city's economic health and the general state of the national economy are essential to accurate assessment of a property.

Your goal is to mushroom you equity into as great an amount as possible. It becomes academic that if you are compounding your equity at each turnover, it is especially important to put as much money to work as possible.

To prove this point, let us use the following chart as a demonstration. We are going to double some numbers ten times.

1	2	3	4	5	6	7	8	9	10
1	2	4	8	16	32	64	128	256	512
3	6	12	24	48	96	192	384	768	1536
4	8	16	32	64	128	256	512	1024	2048

After 10 steps 1 has progressed to 512
3 compounds to 1536
4 compounds to 2048

As illustrated in the chart, if you start out with 3 times as much, you will end up with three times as much (3 x 512 = 1536).

If you start out with 4 times as much you will end up with four times as much. (4 x 512 = 2084).

By pyramiding you are anticipating a series of sales and/or exchanges. In each move you hope to double the value of what you are going into. You may not always achieve this, nor is it necessarily your game plan, but it is something hoped for and often is achievable.

We have illustrated in our chart that by doubling the number four ten times, we'd end up with a total of 2,048. If we were talking about starting our investment with an equity of $4,000 and doubled it 10 times we would pyramid this figure to $2,048,000. Maintaining an equity of 10%, we would have compounded that $4,000 cash to a net worth of $204,800.

35

Remember:

— Use as little of your own money as possible and as much OPM as you can. Be sure the property's income will cover the debt.

— Take as much tax deduction for depreciation as possible as quickly as possible.

— Non-residential buildings are risky investments for inexperienced investors.

It's time to get started and to **buy it right.**

NOTES

Chapter Six

PRINCIPLES OF PYRAMIDING

There are two main concepts that are of paramount importance, 1. to get started; and

2. to start with as much equity and leverage as possible.

Let's take a hypothetical trip through a few progressions to show what can be done*.

Step One

For example let's start with a single family dwelling in an unattractive part of town. It may have been in foreclosure. You probably offered the party a few hundred dollars to *sign off his interest (via a quit claim deed) shortly* before his 90 days were up. (This procedure will be explained in Chapter 8). You undoubtedly have 3-6 months of payments to make up but you're still in for a song.

Spend some time cleaning the place and doing some simple cosmetics — paint, repair, perhaps a cement walk to the steps or door — anything to make the place look better without really spending money.

It is worth some time to visit tract homes. The models are professionally done and you pick up some wonderful ideas that are inexpensive. One such is the use of hanging plants and greenery (either simulated or real) and wall paper or bright colors. These pros understand the psychology of making things feel homey. It costs you little to copy their professional techniques. These ideas can sell and rent you properties.

Now rent this house to someone that will look good on paper. You want top rental money because that makes your property worth more. If you can put somebody in there that will pay like clockwork, you have some saleable merchandise. The government is a good tenant. Let's rent it to a welfare tenant and have her **request** that her rent be sent directly to you.

Now you immediately have something ready to turn over to Step #2.

After acquiring this first property, you also could pick up something similar to this and put them together to boost your equity toward Step 2. This is what I referred to as "grafting".

Anytime you can pick up an additional cheapy, by all means do it. I assure you that by such a practice you will be well on your way to compounding your equity. (At this time, it is debatable as to whether you trade your property or sell. This is the point where I was referring to pruning — we want to look down the road a bit and to get the greatest possible yield we can. More on this in the Appendix E and Chapter 7).

Capitalization

Sound logic tells us that the greater the profit, the higher the market will bring. This is mostly how income property values are calculated. There are formulas predicated upon monthly or annual income — both gross income (without taking out any expenses) and net income (after deducting expenses.) It still comes to the reality that the greater the income, the higher the value of the property.

A prospective buyer is not going to see how much money you took in. He is buying future rent based on the **present rents,** and your history of vacancies and other expenses. Create a chart showing the days your units were filled. It matters not, if the tenants were in there for ½ rent or whatever. You are creating a realistic image for vacancy factor. Through capitalization formulas, if you can prove your vacancy factor is low, you can legitimately get more when you sell. (See Appendix B)

Step Two

That worked so beautifully, let's try it again. We want about 3–4 units. That same part of town is good enough for us. There are apartments available down there through foreclosure — we could perhaps try that one again. We could be looking for this deal while we're still working on Step 1. Tenants in this part of town can be less than ideal, therefore some owners are motivated to get out — this works to your advantage. As long as we have equity, we could perhaps use a broker in the area.

We hope to get into these 3–4 units, cosmetize them, and again put in our clockwork welfare tenants and sell quickly while it physically looks good, and before the tenants want to move. (Just because their payments are being mailed, doesn't make them less fickle. It just looks good on paper to your new buyer).

By this time we're really on our way.

At this point we will graduate into something bigger when we can find something that will carry its own weight without risking everything.

We may have to wait awhile for appreciation to increase our equity.

We could refinance these apartments, and pull out some money to start again with another such "starter" house or perhaps another 3–4 units. If we did, we could possibly lessen the time necessary for our next step.

Step Three

We should be into 8–12 units and we can have units anywhere. Please remember, it is what comes out on paper that is important to you. This is the step that can best be made in buying a run-down apartment from a motivated seller. It is absolutely amazing what paint, carpeting and drapes can do to completely change the appearance of a place. If necessary, borrow a little to purchase carpets and drapes. You could perhaps borrow on your building from the lender (or lenders), but now you are a business person with a sizeable equity. If you have money, you can borrow from a bank. It makes it easier for the next time you need to borrow, so let's establish some credit at your bank.

If you remember the capitalization factor it's important for the market value of your apartments to bring in top rent and have no vacancies. When trying to sell or exchange, be sure to have every unit filled, even if you have to move someone in for a first month free. If that apartment is filled, you count that person as paying.

By now you should be enjoying the advantages of being a landlord. You are not giving as much to the government, you have more to spend, life should be more enjoyable because you **know** where you are going and it is reassuring — it's fun!

It is suggested that by this time you should have acquired a capable, responsible realtor that is sophisticated in tax situations and perhaps some syndication. He will be able to pay his way with you in what he can save you in eventual taxes and in determining what and when to buy.

At this point there are many tempting variations you can attack, but it is strongly advised that you stay in your game plan of residential income property.

Step Four

You should be able to move into 16–24 units. It could perhaps be time for a manager. Your properties and equities should financially be able to take care of themselves with reasonable supervision from you.*

You are working with time, and patience is needed until you can work up your equity. You can do nothing about increasing the inflation factor (leave that to the President!), but you **can** keep your property in good condition physically and from the point of profit — remember what capitalization does?

If you had some equity in some other property to add to

your 16–24 units, you could cut down this interim wait that you're enduring, waiting for your accruing equity to carry into step 5.

Don't forget that anywhere along the way you can start another sequence — perhaps you don't care to start again in the risky part of town, but there are other opportunities to pick up some bargains. Remember now, you have a financial statement and credit established at your bank. You can borrow money any time you find a bargain to buy.

I'd rather not elaborate past step 5. You should be into 30–50 units or possibly into another equally advantageous forms of income property. By the time you're at step 3, I assume you'll be sophisticated enough to know what is going on. You don't even have to be smart, just smart enough to find the right realtor you can trust and who'll take care of you the rest of the way up (it's good for him, too). You two will end up good friends because of the mutually good thing you're doing for each other. To summarize, you can pyramid your way to commercial property wealth by:

1. Locating OPM sources you can use when you find the right property

2. Using appreciated increased values as collateral

3. Borrowing more money based on your appreciated collateral

4. Continuing the pyramid or lever by using yet more borrowed money and increased property values

5. Believing in continued inflation.

**There have been many books written on pyramiding. Two in particular are good and go into detail on buying bargain properties. Nickerson is the patriarch of them all and Haroldson is excellent and elaborates more on financing and refinancing properties. Both should be read, but keeping in mind that they (especially Nickerson) were written some time ago and that many figures just don't hold true anymore and certainly IRS regulations have changed in reference to depreciation and exchanging properties.

*The procedure of buying run down apartments and inexpensively fixing them up will almost always pay you dividends.

**Remember the compounding theory of pyramiding money. One good rule is never to pull out money from equity unless it is to reinvest — live on your earned income or salary.

William Nickerson, "How I turned one thousand into three million in Real Estate in my spare time." Simon and Schuster, New York, 1969.

Mark O. Haroldsen, "How to Wake Up the Financial Genius Inside You" Mark O. Haroldsen Inc., Salt Lake City, Utah, 1977.

Section IV

How to Pluck Your Dollars
Right From the Money Tree

AUCTION ACTION!

Kids sometime start the prank of looking and pointing up into the sky. Soon everyone is looking up. There are several variations, but basically, it tells of crowd psychology.

Merchandise in a retail store could sit for a long time with no action. However, the same merchandise at the same price during a mammoth sale goes quickly. This behavior is evident in auctions.

I have witnessed auctions at van and storage warehouses when unclaimed boxes were sold for overdue storage fees. It can really be wild to see the exorbitant price people bid for a box of which nobody knows the contents. If action is there, people are drawn into it. Conversely even if the property is valuable, if nobody shows interest others are reluctant to join in. Odd, perhaps, but this is what happens and some real values slip through.

Chapter Seven

EXCHANGE VERSUS SELL

A much-used money-maker (and tax shelter) is the trade or exchange. This system depends upon the IRS definition of "like kind", as applied to real estate being exchanged for real estate. The definition of "like kind" is broad. For example, an owner of a commercial building trading for an apartment complex, a corporation trading industrial property for unimproved land and an apartment house owner exchanging for a farm would all qualify. Whether the real estate is productive or unproductive, improved or unimproved; residential, commercial, industrial or agricultural, makes no difference. However, the property can't be held primarily for resale (i.e. dealer property) or a personal residence since these are not considered properties held for investment. When a property is sold and there has been a third party substitution, this is not a legitimate trade but a sale; and, consequently, it will be taxable. When an exchange actually does take place, it is not always nontaxable; it may be partially taxable but nontaxable at present (deferred tax).

That is, when you **sell** your income property for a profit, and it records in the county recorder's office, you owe the government money—even if you take your proceeds and invest them that very same day into some other income property.

If you haven't held the property longer than 12 months*, IRS figures that any profit is included as personal income and is taxed as such. If it has been held beyond that point, you pay tax only on a portion of that **capital gain**.

If that property is exchanged, then it is not currently taxed —it is not tax free, because the government anticipates they'll get their hands on it sooner or later. Let's call an exchange **tax deferred**, not tax exempt. (When the government succeeds it is called **recovery**).

In an exchange situation, whenever any cash is brought out of the transaction and not reinvested, it is called **boot** and is taxable.

However, the IRS gives major tax advantages to real estate owners who want to exchange their properties for larger real estate properties (IRS Code, Section 1031). Because they have heard so much about such advantages, beginning investors often wrongly think tax-free exchanging entitles them to sell their investment property on the open market for cash (without tax) as long as they reinvest the proceeds in larger property within the following eighteen months. Not true. If you sell for cash, you must pay taxes on your profit, no matter what you do with the money. In order to "defer" taxes, you must exchange your equity for a larger piece of property. If you exchange for a smaller property, you may still have to pay taxes; if you receive anything that is not real estate (i.e. cash or personal property), you may also have to pay taxes. However, if you exchange for a property of greater value with a higher total mortgage amount, and do not accept any cash or personal property as payment, you may be eligible for a tax-free exchange. You won't have to pay taxes on your gains until you sell the new property for cash (you could exchange again tax-free) or die. This way, you can defer any taxes you have on the profits from your properties for a lifetime, as long as you obey the rules set down in Section 1031 of the Internal Revenue Code. This leaves you with more money to invest because not only does your real estate shelter a portion of your personal income tax with depreciation, it also shelters your capital gains.

Let us remember what our goal is—we are not primarily aiming at sheltering our income, we are trying to build a large estate. If we take too much depreciation at the early stages, it could effect the shelter when we need it more later on. (For further explanation, see Appendix E on depreciation).

To avoid becoming too complicated, let's just say at this time, it is to our advantage for our purpose of estate building to take just enough depreciation to keep from making profit on paper.

In some older real estate investment books you will find expressions like free exchange. Don't fault the author, tax regulations change and they will change some more. Free advice from the wrong person is no bargain. A fee paid to a tax accountant or attorney is a good investment—get up to date.

How do you find someone who wants to exchange? Any seller may be a potential exchanger. You will find that many sellers are already familiar with exchange advantages—especially the tax advantages; there are even some sellers who will not make a move without exchanging. If you have properties you would like to exchange and can't find an "exchanger", contact your local Board of Realtors to find names of those persons actively engaged in exchanging. In fact, there is no reason to use cash as long as you can find someone who wants your property more than he wants cash for his own. And, not only can you, as the investor, increase your equity dramatically using exchanging; you can also pyramid your holdings from smaller properties into larger ones. The ways and means used to achieve trades are endless.

*The number of months required for capital gains changes from time to time as tax laws are revised.

NOTES

Chapter 8

SOME BARGAINS

A bargain, strictly defined, is the purchase of a property for less than market value. And bargains will continue to exist as long as this country has a free enterprise system because under this system some people will experience financial problems.

That is, through absolutely no fault of their own, responsible, capable, honest, high-calibre people can end up in a financial crisis. A series of combinations of many things can happen. A person could have an illness or injury, or a family death or divorce could happen. Perhaps that person affected could be an employer and he goes bankrupt, thereby pulling some unsuspecting, undeserving person under. A lost government contract or an industry shutting down can chain react in the lives of many secondary families. Weather can affect business: too much rain, not enough rain, too much snow, wind, sun. Unavoidable things can affect our lives financially.

One kind of bargain occurs when for one reason or another people can no longer afford to make payments on their homes and/or need their equity out of them. When a party falls

51

behind on payment, the creditor (trust deed holder) protects himself through FORECLOSURE. He serves legal notice of his intention by filing a "NOTICE OF DEFAULT". The delinquent party then has 90 days to bring his account current before things get worse. Your county recorder's office lists these notices of default, and you can bet there will be more than a few opportunists out attempting to buy up the distressed party's equity (at a fat discount, of course). Because defaults must, according to law, be published prior to foreclosure sale, you have an excellent opportunity to contact the property owner to see if he would be interested in selling his property before he loses everything to foreclosure. Though all bargains found this way may not be ideal, this is one way to find excellent buys at several thousand dollars below true market value.

A fact to keep in mind regarding this kind of transaction is that toward the end of the 90 day period, the delinquent is generally not in a very good position to bargain. He must catch up the whole delinquent amount (including charges and penalties). If he doesn't, he has only 21 days left before he is completely stripped of all interest in the property. In these last 21 days, he must pay off the entire amount of the account **in full** plus penalties and charges. If this isn't taken care of, the property goes to auction (called the trustee sale).

When this trustee sale goes to auction, the trust deed holder has the option to bid the entire amount owed him on paper, and from that point or amount, the auction ensues. Incredibly, sometimes nobody even shows up. Of course, the better the property and the greater the equity, the more activity there is in attendance and bidding.* The sequence of foreclosure is outlined in Appendix G.

At these sales only cash or certified checks are acceptable.

Again, anytime up to that 90 day point, the delinquent party can sell his interest, and the prospective buyer would have to bring the account up to date.

From the lender's viewpoint, the deed of trust is preferred because upon notice of default the debtor has a limited right of reinstatement of the loan but no right of redemption after foreclosure.

Caution — anyone in this much trouble generally has other things that have also slid — he held onto his house tenaciously — other creditors may have successfully sued and put a lien on the house. If that is the case, that lien would have to be satisfied before title could come into the buyer's name.

Another source of "good buys" is the various auctions held for tax arrear properties. These auctions are held yearly by municipalities having tax powers. Brief descriptions of the available properties are advertised in local newspapers.

Auctions can be exciting and the unbelievable is commonplace. Worthless properties are sold for unwarranted high prices — some type of hysteria seems to overtake some people. Sometimes, for unknown reason, valuable property draws little interest and goes for pennies on the dollar.

Because participating in an auction is a tricky venture, it is imperative that you, the prospective bidder, decide upon a final bid before entering the auction. You must discipline yourself not to go beyond your original decision on how much you are willing to pay. If you are outbid, forget the property.

The investor who is diligent, does his research and is prepared (cash, in most cases) will eventually come up with a good buy — especially if he is willing to check in the less glamorous areas.

Some other types of auctions:

Sheriff's sale — when a creditor has taken a debtor to court and has been awarded a judgment, the amount becomes a lien against the property and can actually in some cases, cause the property to be sold at auction. These sales are supposed to be advertised and posted both on the property and in the courthouse.

Some fantastic stories occasionally are heard when $25,000 properties are picked up for car repair bills of a few hundred dollars. Can you spare the time to familiarize yourself with the courthouse posters and such sales?

Tax sale — when the property taxes go unpaid, the property is deeded to the state. The owner can redeem this anytime within a 5 year period by paying the back taxes and a slight penalty. However, after that 5 year period, the property is **eligible** to be sold for taxes. That doesn't automatically mean it will be.

There are many properties in the back country which have been long forgotten, with taxes unpaid. Perhaps the owner died and present-ownership is unknown or those inheriting the property cannot be reached through lost or inadequate addresses. After the five year period, if some citizen requests that this go to auction, then the property will be brought out to the auction block.

Sometimes these property sites are difficult to find and people don't bother to drive around the back country to locate them. These are excellent "starters" or "new starters" as property held with nothing owing gives you great leverage for exchanging.

Do you have time to check with your local tax collector's office for details?

Trustee sales — these have already been covered to some extent. These sales must be advertised in the local paper of circulation (sometimes just the local newspaper, sometimes a city has a "trade" newspaper which posts such sales, notices of fictitious names and the legal notices required by law). People have been competing for 90 days and 21 days for these bargains.

The old pros don't bother with such properties unless there is a husky balance left in it for them. There is still a good margin for your starter. The lesser bargains will still be there — especially if you are willing to go into a riskier part of town.

Administrator sales — when a widow, widower or single person dies without a will (intestate), if there are no survivors (and sometimes when so elected by the survivors), the county is appointed **administrator** to settle the estate and to pay taxes. Your county holds such a sale. This is done periodically where a public auction is held. These attract a lively gathering. The prime properties naturally get an enthused reaction and bidding goes accordingly. However, the lesser properties and the remote properties that are difficult to find, hold some real bargains. The county appraised value is slightly lower than the true market value. The bidder is obliged to start his bidding at 90% of this appraised price. Some bargains will slip through here.

You can find a wealth of bargain-hunting information in your local county courthouse. Legal notices filed on the bulletin board list individuals and companies who have had judgments rendered against them, who have had properties foreclosed or who are behind on their payments. They will also list individuals who are seriously delinquent in paying their property taxes. All of these people want out of their debts; most would welcome your offer to buy. Also, by a phoned request, most county public administrators will put you on their mailing list. (They also auction off vehicles, mobile homes, trailers and many varied personal effects.)

Search the commercial record, a publication that lists not only divorces but judgments, bankruptcies, foreclosures, deaths and probates for the benefit of attorneys and title companies. The commercial record costs as little as $100 annually and can be a very valuable listing. Ask your attorney if he knows about such a publication. Check into the possibility of getting used copies from your attorney or title company. Most public libraries also have copies for us.

Still another way to find bargains is to talk to as many attorneys and accountants as you can. The first person a seller talks to about selling his property is usually his accountant or lawyer.

Pay attention to "For Sale by Owner" signs. Make a habit of stopping and asking the owner about the property and details of the sale. Don't be afraid to stop; the sign on the property indicates the owner welcomes inquiries. Walk in, inspect the property and ask every question you can think of. It's an excellent free education.

If you are a handy person and have the time to fix up property, find a rundown, dirty home that is selling for a price below market value. After locating the rundown property, make a careful inspection and be sure there are no structural problems you cannot handle. Then, make a ridiculously low offer. It may take two or three offers to buy such a home, but when you get one, you can make several thousand dollars with hardly more than a paint brush. Although there are many properties that appear to be a rich find, only close inspection will determine whether you've located a real bargain.

The Ensign Pulver Theory

If an off-color story brings across an important real estate theorum, I assume the strategy excuses the means.

In the movie Mr. Roberts, the outlandish character Ensign Pulver was confiding to Doug Roberts how he fell heir to some girl's virginity. It was simple, he said, nobody before had ever asked her!

I don't necessarily recommend this in social life, but this principle applied to real estate is beautiful. It costs you absolutely nothing to offer—(not even a slap in the face)!

Sooner or later you will fall heir to a real winner. Let's make a few offers!

*Let us assume you have become the successful bidder. You leave a deposit of 10% and generally have 30 days to raise the balance. Most other types of auctions require cash or certified funds for the entire amount. There are many variations of this format.

NOTES

Chapter 9

SOME MORE BARGAINS

Out of Town Ownership

Many times unused property is owned by people out of town. Perhaps they inherited it or had to leave town never to come back. Maybe it is owned by some old folks who will never make use of it. Quite a bit of unused back country property is owned by someone who lives elsewhere. This can also apply to city lots that are unused. This is the perfect time to use your Ensign Pulver Technique—it costs you nothing to make an offer, and if you make enough offers, one will eventurally drop into your hands.

The county recorder's office can be a valuable tool in your hands. The office is required to keep records that can be of great assistance to you:

1. Names alphabetically of all property owners and the addresses to where the tax bills are sent;

2. Property listed by parcel, book and lot number. This also tells you who the owner is and mailing address. It also breaks down that property description to street address (if in the city). Conversely, the street addresses are cross indexed so you can pick up owners by either address or lot number;

3. The date the last property transaction took place.

Executor sales

When an attorney is handling the estate of a deceased client, the property frequently has to be sold to pay taxes and costs (including the attorney's). Any money left over is to be distributed through inheritance distribution. Many different styles are used here—some explicitly legitimate and some rather obscure. However, someone is getting to them—can you?

Trust sales

This is the same operation as an attorney acting as an executor, the difference being that this executor power has been left to an institution—generally a bank. Most banks have a trust department (even if only in the main branch). A routine tour of these officials and getting to know them can pay dividends. Who is the trust officer in your bank?

Divorce

Another good source is the divorce file. Look for recent divorces. Examine the complete files; they tell about property jointly owned and probably available for sale.

Heavy divorce loads in recent years have somewhat altered the procedures. With equal rights and with divorce up, the judges are obliged to point for speedy action and liquid settlements. In the absence of a pre-hearing settlement, the judge more frequently says "sell" and split the leftovers. (In equal rights the man has his rights to community property, too.)

Naturally all the realtors are aware of this too and they are out to compete for the listing as soon as the divorce hits the paper. (This is true also for the death list). However, the realtors rarely follow this up properly. About 45 days after they filed for divorce, the couple has had its day before the judge—then is the time to approach them. The judge has pushed them closer to the sale. Here is another good place for Ensign Pulver Technique.

FHA and VA Resales

The government occasionally forecloses on houses. They bring them up to high condition and then turn around and sell them. (The government takes a licking on this phase, but it's a good deal for the purchaser).

If you qualify by making enough money to fit their formula, you can get into these for extremely low down payments. You are obliged to live in them for a period (subject to change but currently 6 months), but then you're legitimately entitled to sell. Here is another starter. Check the want ads. Some broker is specializing in selling these properties.

NOTES

Section V

Does this Gardener Have Patience?

In 1923 Germany had a spectacular inflationary bust. In order to buy groceries people literally carried their paper money to the market in bushel baskets and wheelbarrows.

I spoke with a German couple who had personally experienced the melee and later came to Southern California where they engaged in Real Estate Purchases.

I asked them who came out best in the rapidly changing times—

1. The person with his home paid off.

2. The person with 50% equity.

3. The highly leverage individual.

The response was immediate and emphatic—the highly leverage person came out best because the balance was paid off with inflated money.

In essence this is what we're experiencing in these times but at a less exaggerated rate. Aren't we trying to pay things off with inflated money?

Chapter Ten

SURVEY OF REAL ESTATE

Let's look at some of the different kinds of real estate in order to select what will be best for you.

Business and Commercial—There is a lot of money to be made in business and commercial property—especially in the development thereof. There is also a lot being lost here. Shopping center developments, economic trends, overloaded areas—there are a good many reasons why any but the experts should steer clear of these investments, and even these get burned.

Farmland—There are some beautiful moves that can be done with groves, especially in Southern California, and Florida, but those are geared more for speculation and tax shelter than building an estate and empire. Somewhere along the line, if you start a second pyramid, you might use that for speculation and perhaps do some good things with it, like buying unimproved land and installing groves. After 2-5 years in this, and subdividing your groves, creating some building sites within a bearing grove, you can do well. There are numerous prosperous such ventures—but that doesn't fit your picture and what you're doing. Remember, you are building an estate.

Raw land—There is money to be made here also. Unimproved property offers two choices. You may purchase the property at below market value and turn it around quickly, selling it at market value (imaginative advertising helps) or

66

look for an opportunity that offers a chance to make a substantial profit in a few years. In order to achieve this profit, it is necessary to purchase a cheap, unimproved parcel, wait several years and then cash in. To do this, look for a parcel that is out of the high-priced land district but in the path of progressive expansion. If you know something that looks like a sure fire return because of a freeway, a shopping center, a manufacturing development—then this can be a windfall, if you know what you're doing.

This type of investment also does not fit your picture, unless again you have started a new project that you can afford to speculate with.

This type of investment is better suited for the long term investor who can invest his money and be patient until the investment matures.

Leverage is not available, nor is other people's money, nor is depreciation (and taxes do go on).

Some Pitfalls

Resort properties are notorious for attracting people to the "ideal" life. The SBA* knows that these are shaky risks as so many quirks of fate affect these up and down business. Resist the temptation, danger lurks here, and many have ventured into the trap and lost everything.

Many will make money on fads and when overbuilt and over-competitive, or the fad passes, many enterprises will lose. Those investors in residential income property will still be pyramiding. (People will always need residential property).

Fads are dangerous. In the 40's miniature golf was popular, in the 50's it was bowling, in the 60's trampolines, in the 70's racquetball and skateboard parks.

Awkward financing can bog you down. If payments are too big and there are too many trust deeds, it can become a difficult task to sell the property. If a property cannot be refinanced, many times the anticipated seller will wait a long time before being able to turn it over. For instance, if your property is substandard for some reason, banks and lending institutions will not lend on it. Some examples to watch out for:

• not connected to water sources (other than well);

• not on paved road;

• access to property through easement only;

• functional obsolescense—like not having a forced air heating system.

The facility of easy financing is most generally the key to selling a property easily.

Taxes—Some common tax pitfalls are:

—If an installment sale is made with 29% cash, it must be remembered that the interest charges on the remaining balance will, during the first year, possibly increase the cash to over 29%. This will destroy a tax advantage.

68

—When cash is involved in a trade situation, that portion is not tax-sheltered.

—Dealers may not be involved in tax-sheltered exchanges.

—Keep in mind that many so-called tax-free shelters are not tax free but tax-deferred.

Residential Income Property

There are many good reasons why you're better off in a residential income property. You have leverage. OPM, depreciation and a guaranteed future market.

Residential properties may generally be divided into categories: new, old and single and multiple family buildings. A single family house is the first property bought by most non-dealer investors. Of all real estate investments, single family rental houses are probably easiest to buy and sell and are useful for tax-deferred exchanges. Most investors who own houses are their own managers—they collect the rents, personally handle whatever problems arise with tenants, keep the books, write the checks for repairs and maintenance or do repairs themselves. This gives them experience in property management and a background for more ambitious realty dealings.

Single family houses have many advantages:

—quite a few are available for no cash down

—maintenance costs are lower

—tenant problems are fewer

—building costs are less

—land taxes are lower

They also have disadvantages:

—they are either fully rented (one family) or fully vacant

—if vacant, you have to make the house payments out of your other income

—some tenants do not stay in single family buildings as long as in multiple family dwellings.

However, a rental house is almost a sure profit-maker if it is located in the path of future growth or wherever housing demand is steady. A survey of neighborhoods can pay off by enabling you to judge whether a house is in a location that should improve or at least stay the same. Don't look at *houses* when you set out to buy—look at *locations*! If you hear about offerings at reasonable prices in locations you haven't yet investigated, check with a realtor to see whether the location is in a good suburb or a growing section of the city. Even if it isn't, perhaps it is at least in the line of growth.

When you buy a one family house, remember that you'll be buying resale value. That is, whoever you resell it to will probably live in it and a buyer will be much more concerned about the location than a renter would be. He'll want a neighborhood that's good for him and his family. Even if you've sized up the locations as "apparently good" (you wouldn't even be thinking of investing there if you hadn't), make sure by talking with people who can give you inside information.

Depending on your talents and spare time, you may or may not evaluate a house in terms of whether you can fix it up. An amateur with building-trade skills can rehabilitate houses and resell at handsome profits, if the neighborhood is right. The money saved by doing the work can make a sizable increase in spendable income as well as resale profit.

Here are some things to remember about single family dwelling purchases:

—The single family home will cost you less to buy than vacant land, commercial real estate or multi-family property. This means that you can pyramid your holdings more quickly.

—Buyers and tenants consider the single family home the most desirable.

—Vacany rates—because of this *demand*—for the single unit home are very low.

—It is primarily *appreciation* that helps bring in yearly profits of 25...50...75...and even 100 percent on each of your invested dollars.

—Because people will always require shelter, real estate—particularly homes—is a very *safe* investment.

—Real estate can be as *liquid* as any other investment. Single family homes are more liquid than any other type of real estate investment; that is, when realistically priced, your house can be sold quickly and converted into ready cash.

—Single family homes are the *easiest* real estate investment to buy, to manage and to sell. Only vacant land offers less management considerations. Rental homes are also subject to less governmental control then multi-unit apartments.

—Single family homes are separate entities with their own tax bases, so you can maneuver properties for almost any desired financial effect. For example, tax-free income in a poor income year or a *tax shield* when you need it.

—In most communities the low-income single family home is not being built fast enough to meet demand. In fact, in some parts of the country such homes are not being built at all because builders prefer to construct larger and more expensive buildings for a greater profit.

The fact that new, inexpensive homes are *scarce* can work to your advantage because few new homes are being built that low to moderate income families can afford to buy, and the demand from both tenants and first-home buyers for inexpensive property grows stronger each day prices are being pushed upwards.

What all this means is that single family home investments are a quick and sure way to make good money in real estate. Investors can earn 50 percent or even 100 percent return each year on money invested in rental homes (the return isn't realized, of course, until the property is sold—but the profit is there for the taking).

Some of the many people who are making money with one family homes seem to be using the same method—conversion. The conversion procedure can be simple if one family dwellings or eight rooms or more are purchased in a low or middle class neighborhood. Some conversion possibilities are to: apartments, rooming houses, offices and condominiums. The first and last possibilities are relatively easy to execute because most of these old homes have two bathrooms, one on the first floor and one on the second floor. The first floor always contains a kitchen. A kitchen can be built on the second floor, with the major cost being hot and cold water lines. Knockdown cabinets are relatively cheap and easy to find. After these are installed, a second-hand electric stove and second-hand refrigerator can be put in. Some houses used for this type of conversion have side halls, which means that two separate entrances can easily be created. A one family dwelling has now converted to a two family dwelling. The so-called retail price for conversions is 50 percent over base cost.

In order to get the maximum financial benefit from a residential property, you need imagination and facts. The options are so many that conversion is often the quickest way to success. For example, office buildings can be changed into apartments and apartments changed into office units; apartments can be remodeled into rooming houses; buildings with lofts and attics can be changed into condominiums; and stores changed into apartments. The foundation for all of these changes is: a prospective investor must investigate to determine community needs—needs that may lead to great profits.

For example, ask about taxes. Don't rely on the general "tax rates" published by the city—they can be misleading.

Real estate taxes often vary greatly for areas in the same metropolis; sometimes assessments differ from one house to the next. Such a difference could change the value of a building by several thousand dollars. Find out the amount of taxes last paid on the property and whether there has been a tax change since then. Ask about *all* local taxes and assessments and not just real estate taxes. In outlying areas this is especially important or you could find yourself assessed extra to pay for new streets, curbs, sidewalks, sewers, etc.

The beginning investor also can't go far wrong in considering apartment income property. Apartments are in demand by renters everywhere because houses are difficult, almost impossible, to find at moderate prices. The number of people living in apartments has been rising steadily for some years.

Generally, you'll want the most units you can buy for the money you can afford to invest, and you'll want to make as small a down payment as possible. Your profit will be the same regardless of how much you put down, but your percentage yield will be bigger with a smaller down payment. The more units in your property, the better off you usually are, unless you plan to manage it yourself. If you're going to do this, you may want to start with a duplex or fourplex and expand as you gain experience. Bigger apartment buildings can bring you more profit per purchase price dollar because overhead and quite a few of the fixed expenses are lower when distributed over more units.

It is best to start with properties you can quickly upgrade and resell. Even improving the management so tenants will be happier and so stay longer can be upgrading. If you already have satisfied tenants, upgrading could mean finding ways to cut unnecessary expenses, thus giving you greater profits.

The Have-not Vacuum

A situation is being created whereby young people cannot afford to buy a home or even a condominium. They lack the down payment. In the years to come it will require greater and greater capital in order to buy into a property. People without an equity won't be able to crack the nut, because they haven't grown with the inflation/appreciation. A vacuum is being created where those now (or shortly) without property will not be able to own property. They will be renters.

The apartment and condominium situation doesn't really get better either. Because of building regulations the builders cannot put as many units in the same space as they used to. It is not as profitable for them to build an apartment—the ratio of cost per unit (largely due to land cost) doesn't invite them to build on the smaller lots zoned for multiple residence. It is profitable for them to build high density only. Even as such, the "have-not vacuum" will reach this level also.

There are many cities and county communities that are having growth expanding problems and subsequently throw on a building moratoriam. If the sewer, water, gas and electric supplies are overburdened, we shall see the cities and counties tightening up more and more on multi-family and high density dwellings. What is this going to do to apartments? The most basic rule in economics is based on supply and demand. The more need for a fixed number of apartments makes a greater demand for them—meaning higher prices for apartments. That also means more appreciation. (Of course, there will also be the need for rental homes too.) Let's get started in residential income property.

*For the importance of the overall success of the US economy, it is important to keep healthy the small business enterprise segment. The Small Business Administration is the Federal government agency for lending to this smaller but important phase of our economy.

When there are droughts, floods, freezes etc., there is an influx of government money to assist the afflicted. For other legitimate reasons also the money is available. The SBA definitely is well aware of what happens in the resort business.

NOTES

Chapter Eleven

REALTORS—HOW TO FIND THE RIGHT ONE

My tax accountant once told me, "If I can't save you the amount I'm asking, don't pay me". I was always happy to pay his bill.

Let's use this same logic with your real estate broker. You can, through effort, wits and gumption get yourself off the ground and pretty well on the way to your goal. By trying to do everything yourself, you may overlook something early in your venture that will cost you thousands of dollars in the future. The tax laws are changed yearly, with the IRS plugging holes here and there. What some book tells you might have been good advice 10 years ago, maybe 5 years or even last year. You need good advice on current laws.

Would you pay $50 to an accountant for an hour's interview? You should look down the road a little way—a person holding a million or two in real estate could find a $50 consultation fee a fantastic bargain if it could save him tens of thousands of dollars. Get yourself well briefed from some expert professional advice—ask questions and find the alternatives—then ask these questions of your realtor—if he doesn't know all the answers, he's not sophisticated enough for you to place your entire future with. (You say he's your friend? Would you let your friend take out your appendix?)

Some of these probes could go like this—

Do I want to sell or exchange my first step?

My 2nd?

My 3rd?

I have a good equity in the apartment I need to turn over. Should I exchange or should I refinance and keep my apartments and take my money out to reinvest in other apartments?

Do I pay my capital gains now? When is the best time and the best way to pay them. (That'll separate the salesmen from the pros).

Believe it or not, the answers are not always the same. Much depends on your income, tax bracket, age, economic stability, etc.

Most good agents have several things in common. For example, a willingness to work more than 40 hours each week, to develop new and better habits, and a desire to make a lot of money. They understand, though, that to do the latter they must provide quality service (without quality service they'll never get repeat business and new referral clients).

Most ineffective sales people are somewhat lazy and so don't make any serious attempts to learn sales techniques; they may want to make good money, but they don't have the motivation of the better agent; although they understand good service means good business, they just don't take the time. To such people, being paid a commission is more important than doing a good job. You can identify poor agents by their casual attitude and/or instant sales pressure whenever a client appears the least interested in buying. If you are not really sure if an agent is effective or ineffective, ask how many sales and listings he has gotten in the past three months. If he's had two or less, watch out.

If you haven't found that honest, hardworking and informed agent yet, try asking a friend or business acquaintance for the name of an agent he is very happy with—then ask for an introduction. Many good agents get more than 75 percent of their business from referrals. If this doesn't work, call a broker in an office you at least suspect will be good and let him know you are looking for an experienced agent to help you. Insist on a good agent with several years experience. A first-rate agent will be able to help you identify the weaknesses and selling points of the property you are considering. Remember, however, that his business is selling, and don't expect him to point out all the weaknesses.

Frequently, if not all the time, you will be exchanging your properties while climbing the pyramidal ladder. Most of the exchanges, certainly the most imaginative exchanges in a modern city, are done by a handful of realtors. Find out who they are—will they have enough time to handle you with what you have in mind? (I should think so).

The following chapter will be spent on syndication. Your realtor should be skilled with these tools as well as tax knowledge. Every advantage in real estate can be magnified by an imaginative and skilled syndicator. I will draw an analogy between an automobile and a syndicator. It can be a tremendous vehicle in the right hands, but disastrous in the wrong hands.

A syndicator should be proud of his track record on each venture. Ask to see some of these records—ask for references—ask other syndicators.

Like an accountant or other realtor, he should be worth his services. However, unfortunately, some syndicators become vultures and really pick a few carcasses clean. They can lock you in so that they are using your money for their own advantage. Check around.*

*I highly recommend "Principles of Real Estate Syndication" by Samuel Freshman. Anyone who is going to let someone else invest and control his money certainly owes it to himself to be well informed.

NOTES

Chapter Twelve

SYNDICATION

Syndication is the investment mode of the future because it offers advantages for all types of investors—big or little, and because people will have to invest with pooled resources to get into anything. (Remember the "have-not" vacuum?)

Syndicating is the joining together of two or more people for investment purposes. This can involve taking property jointly, all the way to incorporation. The most advantageous vehicle for our purposes is the limited partnership.

In the usual partnership, each partner has an equal say in the management of the business. If the business is sued, each partner has equal liability for debts, court awards, etc. In this kind of partnership, each equal partner is called a general partner. In most states a partnership can have as many general partners as it wants or needs. Partnerships of all types are used in real estate activities, but recently, the limited partnership has become very popular because it makes raising money easier, is easy to sell to the investors and gives more control of the business operation.

In a limited partnership you may have two or more general partners and a large number of limited partners. Your limited partners have no voice in the managing of the business, are limited in their liability, are only liable for the amount of money they put into the partnership in the event of a lawsuit, and may obtain major tax advantages from being limited partners.

So, the limited partnership has become a popular way to finance real estate — from one small building to an entire office complex. Because the limited partners contribute money but do not take part in the business operation at all, funds can be raised quickly, the legal requirements are not too complex and business operation problems are few.

As a general partner or syndicator, you don't have to put up a cent of your own; you can get the real estate funds you need without registering stock, without complicated legal documents; quickly and at low cost.

Start now to cultivate partner relationships. Try to have at least three or four partners to use when you need them. If you are careful, you will never have to use your own money for any real estate venture; you will be able to rely on other people to provide all the investment capital you need.

There are two main reasons people form partnerships: your need for money and their desire to earn more than 6 percent on their invested dollars. Treat your partners fairly and you will never have trouble finding people willing to lend you money. If you treat anyone unfairly, word will get around, but it will also get around if you return good profits.

Quite a few people have sizable amounts of money sitting in savings accounts earning 6 percent interest. If you can convince them their returns will be higher if they join with you and invest in real estate, you'll be on your way. There are many ways of influencing partners and forming partnerships, of deciding partners, profits and dissolving partnerships when necessary. Here are a few suggestions:

— Don't form a partnership unless you need to — it can be expensive. If you have adequate funds, experience, time and fortitude to do it yourself, do so.

— Define the partnership carefully at the beginning. Know exactly what each partner will contribute to the partnership; such as cash, equity in other property; ability to borrow money; good credit, and good connections. Obvious contributions you, as syndicator/general partner, could make include time, knowledge and perseverence. Whatever you decide on, get it down in writing and make it specific so that there will be no misunderstandings.

— Maintain maximum control of the partnership. If a partner is limiting you, end the partnership as soon as possible. Don't waste time with a partner who does not understand a good deal when he sees one. A good partnership relationship sometimes takes time to establish, so the best thing to have on your side is a good profit-making track record.

— Keep each partnership on a property-by-property basis. Evaluate each property on its own merits, payout the profits when the property is sold and dissolve the partnership. This will allow you to take advantage of other opportunities. For instance, make sure your partner/s understand that if they run out of money, you are free to look elsewhere for other partners if you run across a good deal.

— Decide initially what you will do if one partner decides to sell out to another. This will prevent misunderstandings.

— Decide at the beginning how you'll divide profits. Negotiate the best arrangement for yourself while still making it attractive for the partners who are willing to put up the money.

— Choose partners carefully, get all terms of partnership in writing and stand behind your investments. Teaming up can provide a good solution to an otherwise troublesome money shortage.

— If a prospective partner seems really reluctant to invest a crucial amount of money, try reducing his fears by putting property in his name. Execute a written agreement with him that whenever the property is sold (since the property is in his name, he alone can make the decision on when to sell), the profits will be split according to the agreement.

— Another reluctant-partner attractor is to agree to pay the partner his profit and invested capital first, after the sale of the property.

The limited partnership is flexible in its structure so as to gear its advantage to the investor. For instance, a young investor has little to put down, but could possibly contribute $50 a month. With ten to twenty such investors, it takes little imagination to see what this could do in the way of leverage.

If retired people banded together in an investment, they could put a larger chunk of capital together in order to come up with spendable income.

A skilled syndicator can mold your needs to the investment.

When banding together, people are compounding their purchasing power. If you have $10,000 to invest by yourself, how much of a bargain can you get? Rarely could you pick up something underpriced by more than $5,000. If you banded together 10 people with $10,000 each, you could move in some directions others can't—you could buy some expensive properties at a trustee sale, a default tax sale, bankruptcy sale and so on. One hundred thousand dollars cash available can frequently buy bargains highly underpriced (especially in acreage). Cash talks, and a good realtor/syndicator can do it for your group.

What do you want a limited partnership to do for you? First, let's realize that all the benefits of real estate investment are still at your disposal within a private limited partnership — appreciation, extreme leverage, OPM, and depreciation. If there are ten such limited partners, each gets 1/10th of the tax loss/gain. A corporation has its depreciation taken out for the corporation entity, is taxed and then distributed to you, where it is then taxed again. The two real advantages are that the limited partnership gets better leverage by banding together, and that you are not involved with management problems. The general partner (generally the syndicator) takes on all management (for a fee, of course).

If you were to set up a limited partnership for your ideal situation, you would look for other investors that had similar goals—long term investment and a desire to put no additional cash into it other than the original investment.

It is extremely important to set this group up correctly and to identify possible problems before they become evident. Some of the items you would want qualified:

1. The limited partners have the right to fire the general partner;

87

2. the limited partners have the right to terminate and liquidate the partnership;

3. to establish the term of the partnership life and renewal thereof.

4. To insure proper motivation to the syndicator.

It is also wise to create proper incentives to the general partner for him to stick to the game plan. We don't want him more motivated to build than to sell (give him a piece of the profit). A good, sincere general partner should have a monetary investment in this also.

With the right man at the helm, there's no limit to what he can do for the group.

How can you find limited partners?

Most limited partners are wealthy people seeking the profits of real estate investing without any of the drawbacks, other than losing a few tax-deductible dollars. You can find such people by looking into local sources such as: the social register, golf and country club member lists, expensive auto dealer lists, county lists of other limited partnership investors and rentable mailing lists of high-income people.

If you have wealthy friends, they may be able to give you the names of other wealthy people who might be interested in buying into your partnership. If you do not have wealthy friends, you'll have to meet some, in the places they usually go. For example, golf clubs, country clubs, yacht clubs, university and college clubs and expensive restaurants.

The key to maximum leverage is, of course, OPM — other people's money! You have to overcome your reluctance to ask people for money. Every person you meet is a potential partner — even your relatives. Most people find it difficult to borrow from a relative. True, this tactic does have its drawbacks and could cause serious problems if anything unprofitable happens, but there are also obvious benefits in that relatives are more likely to lend you money (they know you). Friends and business associates are also fair game. Word travels fast when you make money for yourself and others. Talk about your latest successful ventures with everyone you think is a likely prospect; someone will want to invest a little money. Make sure, though, that you are selective. Remember, too, the seller himself might also be interested. In fact, the seller ends up lending money to the buyer in many real estate transactions by agreeing to let the buyer pay him a portion of the remaining equity over a period of time. The borrowed equity is secured by a mortgage on the property purchased, a mortgage on other property or a personal note. Whenever a seller takes back a second or third mortgage, he is really lending the buyer money.

There are, then, many people looking for good, profitable real estate deals into which they can put their money. By putting one or more good deals together, you can get all the money you need to build new structures, fix up existing properties, buy profitable properties and manage profitable properties. Indeed, for those investors lacking the time to seek investments, you can be of great service as a syndicator.

It is the syndicator to whom investors without too much time for their investments often turn. After the initial investment, the investor receives periodic reports and dividend checks. For the busy or retired investor, this is an excellent way to get the highest return on an investment and to earn real estate profits without the daily operating headaches, save taxes on other income, earn future capital-gain profits and keep excess funds working.

Limited partnerships allow investors to benefit from a real estate project's normal early losses. Investors can deduct their pro rata share of the losses from taxable income, and may *sometimes* receive cash from the partnership in the same year that losses are being written off.

How much money can you raise on a limited partnership? The amount of money you can raise can range from as little as $10,000 to as much as fifty million or more. What you can raise depends on the number of participations offered, the price per participation, the number of participations sold and the selling expenses involved.

How do you form a limited partnership? To form a limited partnership, you must first have the guidance of an attorney. Then, prepare the limited partnership agreement, register it with your county clerk or other responsible official and take the necessary steps to sell participations in the limited partnership. Because you are making a private offering of your limited partnership, you must be very careful not to violate any SEC or state rules and regulations. You should know that in 1961 real estate investment trusts were granted special tax advantages provided they conformed to certain regulations. The Treasury Department is in charge of seeing that these regulations are adhered to. Basically, the rules are as follows:

— 90% of the net income must be paid out to investors

— There must be 100 or more stockholders

— Not more than 50% may be owned by five or more persons

— 75% of the gross income must come from real estate related investments

These real estate investment trusts do well, thus providing small investors with a place to put their money with reasonable safety and many tax advantages.

By assembling a series of limited partnerships, you can easily build a real estate fortune in a few years. And as each limited partnership grows and earns money for its members, you'll find you can sell participations more quickly and with less effort. Remember, though, to use this way to success in real estate investments, you must have the advice of an attorney. Don't try to do it yourself, or you may have legal problems which eat away your profits — both present and future.

So, if you need more money than you can get alone in order to purchase that property, consider letting partners come up with the cash. You'll have to give your partners some of the profits, but a piece of pie is better than no pie at all!

NOTES

92

Section VI

Are You Sure the Tree's Growing?

Is There Another Money Tree Around Here?

You are expected to pick up a bargain to get underway. After you are underway, it is easier for you to obtain money for some of the bargains. You should continuously be sleuthing around for such bargains. These bargains could be new starters for a whole new pyramid, or be offered with your initial prime project to give you more equity and to hurry along your progress to the next successive step. You could also use this new starter for a speculative venture that you could afford to gamble with. Keep digging.

Chapter Thirteen

CAN YOU AFFORD TO MOVE YOUR MONEY TREE?

Remember the story of the goose and the golden egg and the moral that you don't kill the goose that lays the golden egg? Let's compare that with our money tree.

You have been shown where your most lucrative soil is to plant your money tree. You have been shown how to maximize growth and production through using leverage, appreciation, depreciation. You have even been given an illustration of how to graft additional limbs (new starters) to make your tree bear more. Are you going to take risks to kill your golden goose or your money tree? As long as your plant is successful, don't experiment.

In your quest for an estate, it is easy after gaining success several steps down the road, to venture out and leave your plan. You will have the capacity to buy a ski lodge, a fishing lodge, a nursery store, gift shop, a bar, etc., that has always been your desire. Sad numbers have lost everything because of these temptations they knew little about. If a plan is successfully working for you why alter it? Don't leave your game plan. After all, which is more important, taking that little ego trip or making yourself financially secure by creating a wealthy estate. You will have abundance and be able to enjoy almost anything. Stay with the plan. Don't kill your money tree.

NOTES

Chapter Fourteen

PLAN AHEAD

The story is told about one hundred men, all born at the same time and starting life with equal opportunity. Sixty-five years later, at normal retirement age, thirty-two have died, sixty-three are dependent on social security, welfare, or the generosity of friends and relatives, four are living comfortably on their incomes from savings and investments, and one is wealthy.

In a lifetime we all earn a fortune. Which do you choose for yourself — dependence or comfort? For the security you want, it is essential to plan ahead, to know where you are going and to stick to your plan. The difference between the "have-nots" and the "haves" is that those who "have" have a plan. Many athletes, actors, entertainers have made fabulous sums of money and have still ended up broke — Why? **Because they had no plan!** It is not even necessary to scrimp and be miserly all your life as some profess. It is only necessary to get a proper plan under way. (By following the plan and ideas in this book, there are many different ways for you to get started, some even without sacrifices of any kind.)

The first step in forming a successful plan is to define goals. Have you written down your goals? If so, could you find your list right now? How long has it been since you looked at it? Even if it's been a long time, it's not too late to start. You can write them down right now, after considering some simple facts:

— Where you are financially. If you don't know this, how can you get where you want to go? Prepare a realistic financial statement. As you prepare your statement, remember to list everything you have in the way of real estate that you still own. If you work things right, you might still be able to use even bad investments to your advantage. You need to know exactly what you've got.

— Set your financial goal. Whether you're twenty or seventy, you can still make money in real estate.

— Write down your goal. Put it somewhere where you can read it often — at least once a day.

— Decide how you will reach your goal. Even if you're a beginner, you can learn to raise investment capital. You can learn to raise investment capital and how to purchase real estate with little money of your own.

— Give yourself time. Work at it a little each day; invest your time in finding the right properties. All real estate that is well selected and properly maintained will increase in value over time.

As your experience increases, you'll learn how to pyramid your investments if you buy solid real estate in good neighborhoods in growing areas, choose each property carefully, set legal protection, seek help from professionals and have some long-range imagination regarding creative appreciation. Don't be frightened by the magnitude of your goal. Start with one property at a time.

It's still possible to get favorable financing, still possible to avoid down payments and still possible to stay in a lower tax bracket when income jumps. More than ever, an alert investor can clean up in today's real estate market. Once you get a firm grasp of the basics, you can use your imagination and ingenuity and begin inventing improvements in your money-getting methods with each deal you make. Real estate can bring in a safe and steady income for a lifetime because opportunities for investors in real estate are everywhere.

Your biggest barrier is inertia — make yourself get started! It's primarily a mental problem — success or failure is controlled by your own attitudes. Don't get discouraged. Property ownership can bring problems, but most problems will be small. The successful investor will not be discouraged by problems but will learn from them. If you can learn from your mistakes, you will eventually be successful. Stick to the financial goal you have set. Keep your equities in real estate and keep your money moving with bigger and better purchases. You must pyramid to really be successful. Learn everything you can. Especially learn from your own experiences. Don't stop there. Read everything about real estate that you can get your hands on. When you meet someone who is successfully investing in real estate, pick his brains. Find out what other successful people are doing.

If you do this, you will be amazed at how fast your real estate garden will grow. And don't be worried because you don't have a lot of money to invest. You can still reach your investment goals; learn how to do it with little or none of your own money. Don't let anyone convince you that real estate investing is no longer possible unless you have a lot of cash in the bank. Remember that inflation has always been with us and always will be. If you believe this, you see the wisdom in buying as many properties as you can with the smallest down payments possible.

The important point to understand is that **you** decide that you are going to do it and then do it. There is absolutely nothing standing between you and financial security except your own procrastination.

NOTES

Chapter Fifteen

CREATIVE FINANCING

As interest rates soared in late 1980 and early 1981, everybody and his uncle was talking "creative financing", real estate brokers and salesmen, real estate investors and just plain folks who wanted to buy a piece of property but didn't know how they could swing the down payment, let alone handle interest rates of 13%, 14% and higher!

After looking over the final draft of this manual, just prior to a summer 1981 revised printing, it was decided that we add a special updated chapter on creative financing, and more importantly, how to create the favorable conditions that make creative financing possible.

Since many real estate investors, as well as ordinary people, wanting a home for themselves, do not have large sums of cash to buy real estate with huge down payments, or the solid credit required to meet rigid qualifications, creative financing is not just desirable, it is a must!

YOU CAN BUY REAL ESTATE WITH NOTHING DOWN!

Some real estate salesmen will be only too anxious to tell you that you cannot buy real estate without a down payment. "You must have some liquid assets (cash money) to purchase real estate", many well-meaning (maybe!) real estate sales people will quickly tell you. Nothing could be further from the truth. Every day in all sections of these marvelous United States (and no doubt in Canada and elsewhere) many people are acquiring homes, condominiums, vacant land, etc. without spending one penny of their own money as a down payment.

Many real estate sales people don't want to consider real estate transactions that are creatively packaged without substantial cash. The reason is obvious: the women and men who act as agents in the buying and selling of property receive their hot little commissions from the cash money involved in the real estate transactions they help close. I do not begrudge real estate salesmen their commissions. These nice folks can be of great help to you in finding great buys. The good sales people know the real estate market well and deserve the commissions they earn. However, in times of high interest rates and "tight money", they too should be willing to be creative. This can be done if they allow their commissions to be paid via a note or by deferred payment. Seems to me, it is better to receive a commission in some unorthodox fashion rather than to receive no payment at all.

UNDERSTANDING "NOTHING DOWN"

Don't get hung-up on just one definition of "nothing down" as it relates to purchasing real estate.

As already mentioned, nothing down can mean not putting one penny down, in which case the seller would probably be agreeing to carry all the paper on the transaction. Your objective, as an astute investor, should be to buy real estate with little or nothing down. This need not always mean that the seller receives no down payment. What it should mean is that you use little or no money of your own. The down payment can come from someone else.

Motivated sellers (the best kind to deal with!), silent partners or anyone else with capital to lend can help you close a real estate purchase. Lack of money is not your number one concern—creative and positive thinking should be.

FIND OUT WHAT THE SELLER WANTS

It's amazing how many real estate investors overlook an important aspect of a buying situation—what the seller really wants! Many sellers do want cash for other investments; many others desire a "steady income" more than they do lots of front money. Obviously, if you guarantee nice monthly payments to someone who wants steady monthly income, you are more than halfway home to making a deal. Communicate with your potential sellers. Discover the reason behind their selling and what they intend to do with their equity after they sell.

Creative financing should be a two-way street, benefiting both the buyer and the seller. To create the favorable environment for a creative financing buying-selling situation, there must be a willingness on both parties to give and take benefits. If you are buying with little or nothing down, you ought to consider paying a larger total price. Likewise, if you must invest a big chunk of cash to swing the deal, the total price and/or the terms should be favorable.

The astute real property investor can often afford to pay a premium price (market value or even slightly above-market) if he or she can get both attractive terms and a low down payment.

Don't let raw greed get between you and good buying situations. There are times when you can get a deal that gives you everything on a silver platter (little or nothing down, great terms and below-market pricing); however, in most of your buying/selling situations, you will have to play give-and-take—raise the price, lower the terms, etc...

THE ART OF FRIENDLY BUT FIRM NEGOTIATIONS

As mentioned earlier in this manual, negotiating can separate the winners from the pack in real estate dealings. Obviously, one needs only basic negotiating skills when dealing with a highly motivated buyer. The real art of effective negotiating will serve you well in communications with "hardnose" or less motivated sellers (or buyers, when you find yourself the seller).

If the seller is standing pat on his price, you must get favorable terms. When the seller is firm on the terms, you must go for a reduced price. When the seller absolutely refuses to budge on either terms or price, wish him good luck and tell him "goodby".

DON'T BE AN "EAGER BEAVER"

The sharp investor hunts for a motivated seller while never appearing to be motivated buyer. Make it clear to every seller you talk to that his or her property is only "one of many you are looking at". Give the impression that there are several "other properties" just as attractive, or more so, than this one. You might comment during the interview, "excuse me, but I must call Mr. Jackson to tell him I'll be a little late to look over his property". Also, regardless of how good you think price and terms are here, let the sellers know that you think better prices and terms are available elsewhere.

Be certain to find out how long the property has been on the market. Anything over 90 days greatly strengthens your bargaining position. If the property has been offered over 90 days, you could reinforce your position by asking the seller "I wonder why nobody will buy this". If the seller counters by saying "It's not my property, the entire real estate market is slow right now", it would be wise for you to reply "Maybe the market is a little slow, but I have noticed several similar properties sell during the past few months (or weeks)".

You must teach the seller a lesson he may not want to learn. The only reason property doesn't sell within a reasonable period of time (10 weeks or less) is that the price is too high and/or the terms too unflexible. The right price and terms can move any piece of real estate!

TALK "BENEFITS"

Many potentially wonderful transactions are lost because the buyer is not skilled at pointing out the many benefits to the seller. When someone puts property for sale, they obviously want out for one reason or another. It doesn't matter what kind of property you wish to buy (a single family dwelling, rental units, a commercial building, vacant land, etc...). In purchasing it, you are doing the seller a favor, provided that he receives the price and terms he feels comfortable with. To create the conditions for creative financing, you should find out your potential seller's unique position and what his goals and objectives are. Don't be afraid to ask, "What do you plan to do with the equity from this sale?" In so doing, you will discover the benefits your seller hopes to realize.

Knowing this gives you a decided edge. Now, you can look at the entire transaction from a broad viewpoint as you go to work to put together the "perfect package deal" to get you what you want and to motivate the seller to let the deal develop and close.

SUPER NEGOTIATING: BUYING WITHOUT CASH

Negotiation skills will serve you well in all real estate transactions. However, the more cash of your own you have to sweeten the pot, the less it's necessary for you to be a master negotiator. When you decide to purchase real estate without using any of your own money, sharper negotiation skills are most desirable.

You have given several properties careful scrutiny and have found one fantastic piece of property you want badly. You and the seller now sit down for that last crucial round of negotiations. Here's where we separate the men and women from the boys and girls.

Three rules are paramount as you fill out an "offer to buy": (1) Get as low a price as possible before you do anything else; (2) Now, go for a very low down—or no down—deal. Be friendly but firm; (3) Know "the twelve methods of buying and selling estate, where the buyer doesn't pay all cash, which seldom happens.

THE TWELVE METHODS OF BUYING/SELLING REAL ESTATE

(1) Cash to existing mortgage.

(2) Cash down and refinance.

106

(3) Cash down with seller taking back the paper (a contract, second mortgage, etc...).

(4) Some cash plus equity in other property.

(5) Cash plus mortgage on other property.

(6) No cash but equity in other property.

(7) No cash, equity plus mortgage on purchased property.

(8) No cash, equity plus mortgage on other property.

(9) No cash, mortgage on purchased property.

(10) No cash, mortgage on other property.

(11) No cash, wrap-around where seller carries paper, with or without promissory note.

(12) No cash, unsecured note for complete equity.

Now, you can see there are 12 alternatives you and the seller can choose from. The first five involve at least some cash up front, the remaining seven do not.

At the very top of the list is the seller's dream—the buyer buy out his full equity. At the bottom of the list is the buyer's dream—the buyer pays nothing down and doesn't even have to secure his debt. The odds are overwhelming that the buyer and seller will have to work out a compromise and settle on price and terms somewhere between No. 1 and No. 12.

As an aware real estate investor employing proven negotiating strategy, you will be striving to keep the transactions as close to the bottom of the list as possible. Items 6 through 12 require no cash on your (buyer's) part.

Here's another key negotiation tactic that you may have cause to use. If there is something in the body of your offer that you do not want the seller to notice, use the "smokescreen tactic", some outlandish point that will capture his or her attention, thereby diverting attention to the point you would like overlooked.

For instance, if you do not want the buyer to focus in on the low price you're offering or the great terms (little or absolutely nothing down), you may list as a condition of sale that the seller paint the house or apartment building, re-landscape the grounds or replace all the carpets. This technique will often have him strongly reacting to this wild clause at the expense of his haggling over others. "Paint it yourself," "Do your own darn landscaping" or "You'll get no carpeting from me" would be likely responses. After a little verbal fencing, you can sigh loudly, roll your eyes to the heavens and explain "All right, these improvements (paint, landscaping, carpeting or anything else) are still another expense I'll handle myself".

You will be surprised if your seller agrees to the improvements as well as the great price and/or terms (but try not to show it!). It actually happens in rare occassions. More often than not, the "smokescreen" will be shot down. So what, as long as you achieve your true objective.

Here are some other "sneaky" but effective "smokescreens":

- Seller must replace the kitchen sink, stove, etc.

- Seller must install a microwave oven.

- Seller must pay all closing costs.

- Seller must relinquish all of his tax impounds.

- Seller must pay all FHA or VA points.

- Seller must pay for a new sprinkler system.

- Seller must remodel the bathroom, den, etc.

- Seller must fence or re-fence the yard.

OFFERS AND COUNTER-OFFERS

Only rarely will a real estate transaction be acceptable at the time of the original offer. In most cases, several offers and counter-offers will be presented before everyone concerned signs on the dotted line. If you're dealing with a real estate broker or salesman, you can expect her or him to have all the necessary forms with them. When working with an agent, you will be relieved of the responsibility of handling all of the needed paperwork. Real estate sales people earn their commissions from bringing buyers and sellers together and by following this up, by taking care of all the details and paperwork.

If you are not working with a qualified real estate agent, guess who inherits this responsibility? Visit a large office supply store and purchase a handful of "Offers to Purchase Real

Estate" forms. Most stores sell these for around 10¢ each or 25 to 50 of them bound into a tablet for a few dollars per tablet. Have these valuable forms with you at all times. You never know when you will need them, and you cannot create the conditions for creative financing without the proper vehicle (these forms) at your ready disposal.

Once you have made an offer and it has been flatly rejected or rejected and then a counter-offer made, you will have to decide if you want to make a new offer. Whenever any conditions of an offer have been rejected, that offer is void and a new offer must be submitted if dealings are to continue. The same form (Offer to Purchase Real Estate) can be used to make another counter-offer, which in fact is simply a new offer.

UNDERSTANDING "PAPER"

If you expect to become a knowledgeable real estate investor who understands the concept of creative financing, you had better familiarize yourself with "paper". Paper, in real estate slang, refers to notes and mortgages, secured or unsecured, by real estate or other collateral. "Hard paper" comes from banks, savings and loans and other established lending institutions; "soft paper" (usually with more flexible terms) are notes obtainable from individuals.

When you buy real estate and the seller agrees to take back most or all of the paper, you are using the soft paper concept to its highest advantage. Savings and loans and banks do business and lend money under rigid terms and conditions. When Sam Seller agrees to sell you his property and is willing to carry the paper, the terms and conditions can be as flexible as you and Mr. Seller wish to make them. In 99 out of 100 cases, you will get a far better deal from an individual than a lending institution. One major exception would be those fringe-type characters who lend cash money and charge huge interest (often as high as 40% or 50%) for the service. Regardless of how good the deal appears to be, and how badly you may need cash, I strongly urge you not to do business with a loan shark. You will pay far too much for the money you rent, and if you should miss a payment, you could be in hot water. Loan sharking is illegal, but there are still several of these unsavory types around. Deal only with individuals who offer money at reasonable rates. Whenever possible, have the seller carry all or part of the paper.

Whenever you obtain real estate with little money down, there will be paper involved. The smart use of paper can create the right conditions of creative financing.

Let's start with notes. When you give your note, for your best interests, the note should be:

(A) Unsecured by any collateral, if possible.

(B) Negotiated at the most favorable interest rate.

(C) Negotiated for the longest term possible.

(D) Negotiated at the lowest monthly terms.

(E) Should not involve a pre-payment penalty.

The art of using O.P.M. (Other Peoples Money) and using paper in a creative fashion is to go into debt only when you can defer the obligation to repay as far into the future as possible. In this way, double-digit inflation works for you, not against you.

Always think in terms of "low and long" as you put together a real estate transaction:

- Low interest

- Low monthly payments

- Long term to payoff

Always start at the bottom and reluctantly work up—inch by inch—negotiating hard every inch of the way. Know your "no deal" cutoff point. Be prepared to walk away from any deal that rises above your low interest or low payment cutoff point. Also, the longer the payback terms, the better off you will be.

High interest rates, high payments and a short term payoff can destroy your fledging financial ship. Let's learn the right thing to do by learning from an investor who did the wrong thing:

Johnny Buyer is new to real estate investing. He is eager to build a substantial portfolio, starting from scratch. So far so good. John locates a nice eight-unit apartment building selling for $160,000. The seller is highly motivated to be rid of his building but needs $10,000 in cash as soon as possible. The seller's existing first mortgage of $120,000 is payable at $1,050 per month; the seller wants to receive the balance of his $30,000 equity over a seven-year period at 10 percent interest, secured by a second mortgage (trust deed on the property. Payments would then be approximately $500 per month.

Johnny Buyer is chomping at the bit; he wants this building, and quickly! In his joy at what appears to be a fantastic deal, Johnny ceases to negotiate and quickly signs the earnest money receipt. He arranges a $10,000 low-interest, six-month loan from his favorite rich uncle and jumps into the transaction.

The transaction closes. Johnny, unfortunately, has not done his homework well. The seller told our Mr. Buyer that rents were $300 per unit and expenses were "around $500 total". Johnny soon discovers the stark naked facts: three of the eight units rent for only $250, another one at $275, three are at $300 and one has just become vacant. Expenses average $750 per month, not $500, and our friend Johhny is looking at a big gap—called "negative cash flow"—even though he does rent the vacant apartment for $300. Here is the math:

Monthly gross rent $2,000
Monthly expenses ....($ 750)
First mortgage payment ....($1,050)
Second mortgage payment ....($ 500)
Monthly negative cash flow ....($ 300)

Johnny finds it very difficult to cope with this $300 per month negative cash flow, but by cutting his living expenses to the bone and with small loans from friends and relatives, he manages to come up with an extra $1,800 over six months.

Suddenly Johnny Buyer's six-month note is due and favorite uncle wants his money—now! He has learned a hard lesson. A short-term loan can lead to financial suicide. If he doesn't want to sell the building or lose it by default, he must borrow money from some other source or sell something he owns to raise capital quickly. Even if he convinces his old Uncle Joe to cancel the balloon payment and accept monthly payments over ten years at 10% interest, that sum of $132.20 per month, added to his current negative cash flow of $300, adds up to $432.20 per month, far too much money for his limited budget.

John is forced to sell, quickly. From a sharp buyer, he now is a worried, highly-motivated seller, ready to unload and any terms that get the "negative cash-flow monkey" off his back.

There are several sure-fire positive ways to attack negative cash flow. For starters, cut the seller's price. If you cannot accomplish this, you should carefully scrutinize the rentals to determine if they can stand reasonable increases once you assume ownership. And how long will it take to raise rents to a point where negative cash is no longer a problem? And until such time as you kiss negative cash flow goodby, can you afford to feed the big hungry cookie monster? And, is the monster a cute little nibbling monkey or a raging, profit-stealing giant?

These are questions you ask yourself, and answer, before you sign into the deal. A short period of time spent with paper, pencil and calculator ought to make things very clear to you.

Now, let's see how our friend, Johnny Buyer, perhaps could have entered his transaction and stuck around long enough to reap a nice profit.

Here are some creative ways to use paper that John may have used:

(A) After going for the lowest total price the seller would accept, he could have obtained his $10,000 loan to give to the seller, but then insisted on monthly payments no greater than gross receivables from rentals. To uncover this sum, he should have (with the help of a competent accountant) looked over the records pertaining to rent payments. Further, he should have directly talked to his potential future renters to confirm the exact amount each paid for their apartment and what services, if any, they expected in return. Aside from determining the precise amount he would be receiving in monthly rents, it is just plain good business to get to know the people who will be living under your roof. One more point: if the building has a history of a 10% average vacancy, you will want to consider this as you set up a payment schedule with the seller.

(B) Setting up the right kind of "balloon payment". The only type of balloon payment that serves the best interest of a sharp real estate investor is one that does not quickly sneak-up and attack him. Instead of an early six month balloon, Mr. Buyer should have worked Uncle Joe for a two or three year balloon payment. This would have afforded plenty of time to improve his property and sell it for a profit or keep it and still have plenty of time to make arrangements to handle the big payback.

(C) After making a $10,000 down-payment, Mr. Buyer could have pushed for yearly payments (instead of a monthly payment schedule). Once-per-year payments are seldom acceptable to sellers of a single family dwellings, but they are not uncommon in the sale of multiple dwellings. Johnny Buyer could have suggested monthly payments on the interest of 10% or even agreed to an increase in interest of 11% to 14% with the principle payable once a year. The first payment, one year from the time he put his (I should say, his uncle's) $10,000 down. This becomes a balloon but buys our buyer one full year in time in order to meet his obligation.

If the seller would have accepted any of the above three terms, Mr. Buyer would have made a good buy (assuming that everything else checked out) rather than a mistake.

It is better to pass up a deal than to plunge in blindly and then realize your error. Negative cash flow is the enemy of all real estate investors. Let's look into a unique method Donna Dedrick of San Diego used to turn negative cash flow into positive results.

Donna recently bought a small two bedroom condo in El Cajon, California (18 miles east of San Diego) for $62,000 from a Navy couple who were eager to sell after the husband was transferred to Baltimore, Maryland. Ms. Dedrick purchased this unit from highly motivated sellers at $10,000 below current market value. Her down-payment was small, and she assumed a low 9% VA loan. Now, all she needed was the right people to live under her newly purchased roof. The only fly in the ointment was the amount of rent she could get. $450 rent per month was as high as the market would bear. Trouble was, her mortgage payment was $625, which represented a $175 monthly negative cash flow. Using the Profit Ideas approach to creative financing, "good ideas are our number one resource", Donna discovered the perfect technique to end her negative cash woes.

Here's how this sharp lady did it:

Ms. Dedrick advertised for her tenants with a "Rent to Own" newspaper ad. After screening several applicants, she found a young couple who accepted the following creative terms:

Rent to own tenants agreed to pay $625 per month (the complete mortgage payment) for the full term of their two year lease-option. At anytime during these twenty-four months, they could exercise their option and buy the condo at appraised value (remember, Donna had bought substantially below market value), in which case $175 of each $650 monthly payment would apply towards their down-payment. If they decided not to buy, the contract called for a refund of $4,200 ($175 x 24) in excess payments they would have made, plus 10% interest. The young couple were pleased with these terms. They would benefit either way. (A) They would be forced to save money at an interest rate above what most savings institutions paid or (B) they would be able to own their own home with a nice hunk of the down-payment ready to apply.

Pat Cavanaugh Long Beach, California, tells the story of how he was a little short of the necessary money to apply as a down-payment to the six-unit apartment building he wished to buy. The sellers were getting a divorce, and this prompted a quick sale at a below market price and great terms. Still, they wanted $15,000 down, and Pat could only raise $11,000. In getting to know the sellers, Rudy and Barbara, Buyer Pat discovered Rudy needed $7,000 to make a down-payment on a house he wanted to buy. Barbara, on the other hand, was uninterested in buying real estate and was quite happy in the apartment in this building that Rudy and she had lived in for

117

four years. Pat Cavanaugh got a creative idea that pleased his sellers. He would pay them $11,000 down. Rudy would take his half ($7,500) of the down-payment in cash so he could buy the property he wanted. Barbara would receive the balance of Pat's down-payment of $11,000 ($3,500) in cash, and in lieu of the other $4,000, she agreed to keep her apartment in the building, granted a full year lease without rent. She was only too happy to accept these terms. Since the going rate for rentals in this building was $400 per month, she would get 12 months of rent for the price of 10! Buyer Pat was only too elated. His creative suggestion, which was accepted, allowed him to buy an excellent piece of income-producing real estate.

Ask questions...get details...think creative! Make suggestions and new offers...it pays handsome dividends!

Good buying opportunities are everywhere (well, almost). We are only limited by the use of our own creative mental powers. Good ideas are still more valuable than money.

As author Napoleon Hill so aptly put in his classic bestseller "Think and Grow Rich"..."Whatever the mind of man can conceive and believe, he can achieve". Amen!

THE EFFECTIVE USE OF PARTNERS

When you run out of money before you run out of super buys (this can easily happen), it is time to consider taking on one or more partners.

Think and Grow Rich by Napoleon Hill (c) 1960 by Napoleon Hill Foundation, a South Carolina Corporation. Also available as a Fawcett paperback.

Since not all partnerships are made in heaven, it is wise to shop around for a suitable partner in the same fashion that you would hunt for a good tenant in a building you owned. Start by actively cultivating suitable partner relationships. Try to build a "stable" of good potential partners to have ready when the need arises. While "greed and need" may be the basis of several partnerships, I strongly suggest you form liaison with men and women who you can trust and respect and who feel the same way towards you. Honesty and fairness from all parties is the foundation of a successful partnership.

If you can show people with money that you possess real skill at finding real estate bargains, you will not have to use your own capital for investing. There are many thousands of people out there with countless millions in low-yield financial institutions who are eager to invest in a real estate transaction that promises big rewards.

By treating your partners well and helping them make juicy profits, you can soon expect increasing numbers of financial backers eager to invest with your next new-found opportunity. Likewise, if you cheat your partner, word will spread quickly, and a good source of capital will dry up.

Here are seven rules concerning the effective use of partners:

(1) Don't bring in partners unless you absolutely must. If you have the necessary funds, time and ability and have uncovered a great real estate buy, why share the profits unless you have to? When you must, choose honorable people.

(2) Make darn sure from square one that everyone involved

knows what is expected (in terms of time, talent and money) of each other. Lay the cards face up on the table. Even honorable, well-intentioned partners can run into a real bugaboo and misconceptions based on poor communications.

(3) Keep as much control of the deal as you can. The very nature of a partnership will restrict your freedom and action (ask any married man or woman!) to some degree. Just make sure there is a limit you will not go beyond. The less control you have, the less advantageous the partnership becomes.

(4) Lay down guidelines in advance—what plan will be followed should one partner wish to sell out to another.

(5) Establish early what procedure will be followed if one (or more) partners do not perform in the fashion he or she has agreed to.

(6) Keep all partnerships on a property-by-property basis. Each project should stand on its own merits. It may be ok for all concerned to take their profits out of one transaction and plow them into another, but not until the guidelines for the new investment have been fully defined.

(7) Decide (also at the time the partnership is being set up) exactly how profits will be allocated. Make the best deal you can for yourself while allowing your partner(s) to share in the profits.

CREATIVE EXCHANGING

More and more Americans are turning to barter as a means of doing business without cash and with small tax consequences. For example, an electrictian may rewire the house of a plumber in return for remodeling a bathroom and installing new fixtures. When two or more people get what they want, it is called exchanging. You can make profitable use of creative exchange in your real estate dealings. Here's one illustration of how it can work:

Terrance Jackson of La Jolla owns a beautiful acre and a half in the California mountains near Julian. Mr. Jackson bought this site for both investment reasons and also with the possibility of building "a second home" someday. Recently married, Mr. Jackson's new wife Jenny is not interested in a mountain retreat but would like to move just three blocks from where they now live to a beautiful home for sale overlooking the vast Pacific Ocean. Mr. Jackson knows the folks who own this ocean view house, Mr. & Mrs. Burt Kirkpatrick. As fate would have it, the Kirkpatrick's are very interested in buying or building a country home in order to "have a place to come home to" in-between worldwide travels, which is their true love. Mr. & Mrs. Jackson strike a deal with Mr. & Mrs. Kirkpatrick. The mountain property in Julian is valued at $75,000, while the ocean view home in La Jolla is valued at $300,000. Mr. Jackson uses his equity of $50,000 in the mountain as the down-payment, reaches agreement to have Mr. & Mrs. Kirkpatrick take back a large ($140,000) second on their home at 12% interest and assumes the low-interest (6%) on the first. Burt Kirkpatrick is delighted with the deal. He and his wife have no need of more cash right now (a large portion of which would go to Uncle Sam in the form of taxes). The steady income from the 12% second mortgage (trust deed) serves their purpose fine. As for Mr. & Mrs. Jackson, they received everything they wanted— and more. By keeping their present house as a rental, they have come out of the deal smelling like a rose.

The above illustration was of a simple two-way exchange. Now, here is how it can work when you're working with a three-way exchange:

John and Cindy bought a small one-bedroom condo in a fashionable area of Fort Worth, Texas, soon after they married in 1978. Now, three years and two children later, they have long since run out of space. John has a friend, Bob, who has just put his home on the market for $65,000. It is a nice home in a good neighborhood, and above all, has three good-sized bedrooms! Bob's home is priced at $65,000 and has a loan of $47,000. John and Cindy's small condo is worth $49,000 with a loan on it of $40,000. Since John and Cindy are $9,000 short of Bob's amount of equity but do not have that sum in cash, some creative financing was called for. Since John and Cindy will owner/occupy the house, they plan to refinance, qualifying for a 90% owner/occupied loan.

The exchange and new financing appear to be solving the problem when out of the blue Bob throws a monkey-wrench into the potential transaction. Old Bob, after due consideration, decides he doesn't want to live in a small condo. Now what? Well, John is a creative guy, and he comes up with the right solution. He brings in a third party, Dick and Mary, who agree to buy the one-bedroom condo from Bob as soon as he receives it on the exchange. The third party (Dick and Mary) will pay $49,000 for it. The $9,000 equity in the condominium is given as a note secured by the condo with a payment of $1,000 in six months and the rest amortized over a two-year period with payments of $100 monthly and a balloon payment due after 24 months. The seller agreed to the three-way exchange, and everyone got what they wanted.

As an alert, creative investor, you can use exchanging to solve many of your real estate investment problems. Not only can you increase your equity dramatically by exchanging, you can also pyramid your holdings. By "trading up" (exchanging small properties for larger ones) you will pyramid yourself to real wealth. You can get started with just one small house or condominium that is priced below market and perhaps needs a little "fixing up". Once equity is improved, the search is on for a bigger and better piece of property (perhaps a duplex), and the process is repeated over and over until you are no longer a small investor but a person with up to one million dollars or more in real estate holdings. You can do it, and faster than you think. Mark O. Haroldsen, William Nickerson, Vince Bartolone and thousands of other creative folks, including the vast majority who receive no publicity and want it that way, have gone from near zero to millionaire status in less than five years. Why not you? If you think you can, no one will be able to stop you!

Exchange is simply another tool in the arsenal of the man or woman who seeks creative means to invest in real estate.

MILLION DOLLAR DEALS ARE ALSO SUBJECT TO CREATIVE FINANCING

Most of the illustrations in this book have concerned creating the conditions for creative financing as it applies to relatively small purchases. This is keeping with the principle, "You walk before you run". However, some of my readers may want to do some "leap-frogging". Rather than question this technique, I encourage it. Just make sure you know what you're jumping into!

123

Here's a great example of what a gentleman named George did in the area of no-money down, million dollar financing:

George discovered a commercial building in Minneapolis, Minnesota. It was priced an even one million dollars. The building was fifty years old but in better constructural condition than many new structures. All it was begging for was 90 or 100 gallons of paint, expertly applied. The rundown condition was hurting business rentals. Three out of the seven retail shops on the first floor were unrented. Both the second and third floors were vacant, except for two hippy-type artists who paid the ridiculously low rent of $75 for one-half of the third floor.

More important than the profile of the big 77,000 square foot building was the profile of its owner. Henry was a easy-going gentleman of seventy-four years and anxious to sell. Weak management had held the rentals down to $80,000 per year. The expenses were also $80,000 per year, so poor ol Henry (actually the older gentleman was quite wealthy) was at a quid pro quo as far as he and his building were concerned. Henry wanted one million dollars for it. He frankly admitted the low amount he was receiving in rentals didn't justify his asking price; however, he pointed out to George the large amount of vacancies and the site's future potential for positive reinforcement. George knew all about this—that's why he was seeking ownership of the building.

It was time George injected creativity into this transaction, and boy oh boy, did he...

George asked Henry how he intended to invest his money if he sold his building. "In mortgages" was the answer. George quickly pointed out that taxes on a million dollars for Henry would likely be around a quarter-million dollars. This fact, which he knew was true, bothered Henry and made him more receptive to George's proposal. Here are the details of George's creative offer:

George asked for a fifty-year lease on the basis of $1,000,000 capitalization at 4% or $40,000 yearly. This is $40,000 more than Henry is currently receiving on his property, since his current expenses are similar to income. Henry will only have to pay taxes on this $40,000 yearly payment. Henry pays no tax on what is actually the sale of the building. Henry is in effect selling the building for a million dollars and simultaneously investing it with George at 4%, using his own building as collateral. This deal offers distinct advantages to both parties. Henry agreed to sell under these conditions.

George has a plan that will make the deal sweet from his side of the investment. He plans to spend $30,000 for paint and other minor, but important value-increasing cosmetics. In return, he expects to bring the total rentals of the three floors to $160,000 or more per year. Thus, after his $40,000 yearly payment to Henry, his $30,000 in cosmetic changes, his $80,000 in expenses, he still expects a positive cash flow of $10,000 for his first year of no-money down ownership of a million dollars worth of real estate. In his second year of ownership, he can look forward to up to $40,000 in positive cash flow if everything works out as well as George planned.

Important Note: In all your real estate transactions, and especially in property worth several hundreds of thousands or one million dollars or more, be conservative when you figure potential cash flow. In the deal outlined above, George pen-

125

ciled in $160,000 as the rental figure he hoped to achieve. In reality, he did even better. He filled up all seven retail units on the ground floor and obtained a major wholesale firm to rent both the second and third floors. Thus, his total rentals reached $175,000 his first year. His expenses, too, were a little higher than he expected—he had to spend around $3,000 to advertise for tenants and also had a few other smaller miscellaneous expenses. At the close of his first year of ownership, his gross profit was $15,500. A fantastic positive return in the first year on a deal of this size. Creative financing personified!

YOUR ABILITY TO FIND CREATIVE FINANCING IS ONLY DEPENDENT ON YOUR ABILITY TO THINK CREATIVELY!

After reading this chapter on creative financing, I just hope one point takes precedence over all others: You will never run out of ways to find and use creative financing in the buying and selling of real estate as long as you cultivate your ability to think creatively.

Ernest Holmes, in his great metaphysical masterpiece, The Science of Mind, states, "everything begins in mind". And so it is.

If you're the kind of person who believes there is an answer to every problem, and who thinks of problems as challenges, your creativeness can make you very rich by investing in selective real estate.

GO FOR IT!

The Science of Mind by Ernest Holmes, Dodd-Mead (c) 1938.

NOTES

127

Chapter 16

HOW TO TAX SHELTER YOUR REAL ESTATE PROFITS

HOW TO TAX SHELTER
YOUR REAL ESTATE PROFITS

Real estate investing may be the very best method to strike it rich in America or Canada. Most millionaires list selective real estate speculation as the road that took them to financial independence. After looking over this informative manual, you may be anxious to go after the big bucks available to the sharp real estate investor, or perhaps you already have acquired a portfolio of real estate investments and now want to increase your holdings. Great! But please look over and digest this valuable information before you go one step further.

Some details on how to shelter, reduce and/or completely eliminate your tax obligation have already been pointed out in the previous text. In this special report we are going to go into greater detail and give you the in-depth legal tactics and techniques that can save you a bundle.

WHAT IS A TAX SHELTER
AND WHY ARE THEY PERMITTED

A legal tax shelter (and the legal type shelters are the only kind we recommend anyone use!) is a means of deferring, lowering or eliminating altogether a tax obligation. The government realizes how important real estate and the entire building industry is to our national economic position. New construction of residential, commercial and industrial buildings is the largest fabrication industry in the nation. The government knows it must give real estate investors tempting incentives to keep billions of dollars of speculative capital flowing into this vital marketplace. Tax shelters are the main incentive offered investors. The leading tax shelters are:

129

(1) DEPRECIATION
(2) CAPITAL GAINS
(3) TAX FREE EXCHANGES
(4) INSTALLMENT SELLING

DEPRECIATION

Depreciation is the reduction in value of property that is not being used for personal purposes. Stock in trade, various inventories, land apart from the improvement and depletable natural resources are not depreciable. There are many depreciable assets to most income-producing properties. All have varying economic lives as regulated by law. The IRS Code lists the economic-life assignments for depreciable assets. The economic life is a subjective assessment by any legal taxing body. The economic life span of any given property may or may not actually correspond with how long it remains an income-producing entity. An apartment building may stand in daily use for up to 100 years (there are many 100 years old and older everywhere in America, especially in places like New York, Philadelphia, Boston, Providence and other major cities), yet the average economic life for an apartment building is usually listed at 25 to 50 years. An office copying machine may be given an economic life of only 2½ years and still be functioning very well after 5 years or more. Don't mistake the taxing advantage of an economic life span with actual functioning ability.

Here is a list of Group One (Buildings) guidelines as listed in a general IRS procedure manual:

```
Apartments  . . . . . . . . . . . . . . . . . . . . . . .  40 Years
Dwellings  . . . . . . . . . . . . . . . . . . . . . . . .  45 Years
Factories . . . . . . . . . . . . . . . . . . . . . . . . .  45 Years
Garages . . . . . . . . . . . . . . . . . . . . . . . . . .  45 Years
Hotels  . . . . . . . . . . . . . . . . . . . . . . . . . . .  40 Years
Loft Buildings  . . . . . . . . . . . . . . . . . . . . .  50 Years
Office Buildings . . . . . . . . . . . . . . . . . . . .  45 Years
Stores  . . . . . . . . . . . . . . . . . . . . . . . . . . .  60 Years
Warehouses  . . . . . . . . . . . . . . . . . . . . . . .  60 Years
Motels . . . . . . . . . . . . . . . . . . . . . . . . . . .  25 Years
Shopping Centers  . . . . . . . . . . . . . . . . . . .  30 Years
Warehouses  . . . . . . . . . . . . . . . . . . . . . . .  30 Years
```

Accurate use of depreciation factors include:

    the amount to be depreciated
    the economic and useful life
    the methods of depreciation
    the tax savings results of depreciation
    using depreciation as an effective selling tool.

Every consideration should begin with a determination of the value of any given building with its improvements. Since the land cannot be depreciated, all calculations are centered around the structure. The simple method for an existing property is to use the current tax bill. This will help you decide what is the value between the land the building(s).

Under current tax laws there are several methods of depreciating income-producing property, but the basis should be determined by cost of improvement to the building, the useful life of the improvement. You can depreciate by (a) Straight line or (b) Declining balance (accelerated methods).

(1)   125 percent declining
(2)   150 percent declining
(3)   200 percent declining
(c) Sum of the Year-digits (the unaccelerated method).

You may Straight-Line any depreciable property. This method is simple and most commonly used. It assumes that the depreciation is uniform throughout the useful life of the property. For example: a property worth $200,000.00 with a 40 year economic life would be depreciated 2½% ($5,000.00) per year, using the straight line method. Simple to use it is, but it is definitely NOT the most advantageous. In most cases, straight-line depreciation gives you the least effective tax shelter.

The 125 percent declining method is 1.25 the straight-line rate and is applied to decreasing amounts each year and not to the original cost. Using the previous example, the 125 percent method would render a $6,250.00 depreciation the first year.

$5,000.00 straight-line method
x   1.25
───────────
$6,250.00

For the second year, $6,250.00 would be substracted from the $200,000.00 cost, and we would multiply 2½% of new balance ($193,750.00), which would be $4,845.00 x 1.25. That would give us a $6,056.25 depreciation for the second year, etc. . .

The 150 percent declining balance method is the same as with the 125 percent rate method, except the straight-line is multiplied by 1.50 in place of 1.25, and the 200 percent method is exactly like the 1.25 and 1.50 methods, except you would be multiplying by 2 instead of 1.25 or 1.50.

In using the Sum of the Years method, changing fractions are applied each year to the original cost (or other basis), less any salvage. This accelerated method is only available on new property. The numerator here is the fraction you apply to the cost of your property and the remaining useful years. The denominator is the sum of the years of useful life at the time of acquisition. For a five-year asset, the denominator would be 15 (1 plus 2 plus 3 plus 4 plus 5); depreciation for the first year would be 5/15 of the cost; for the second year 4/15; etc. On our 40 year example:

   <u>40</u> (last year of useful life)

   820 (the sum of the years-digit)

followed by: 39/820 the second year and 38/820 the third year, etc.

TAX FREE EXCHANGING

Perhaps the biggest, best, most exclusive and most profitable tax-saving opportunity available to the real estate investor is the Tax-Free swap! Should you desire to own someone else's property and should they wish to have one that you own, it is quite easy for you both to get what you want without getting hit by the tax man. The laws require the trade be for like-kind property, but they are very flexible. As long as you swap investment or business property for other similar holdings, you qualify for an exchange of like-kind property when, for example, you swap an apartment building for retail commercial building. Even unimproved land, in many cases, can be traded for various investment and business buildings.

This big tax break is a major consideration for the investor who wishes to sell a property he owns to get cash to purchase another holding. Should he first sell his property, he must pay a tax on his profit. But, if he arranges a swap to obtain the other property, he can use total value of his property because there will be no tax required.

Swapping is another important way to increase real estate depreciation recapture. A two-party swap is very easy to arrange. All we need is any two people who have somewhat similar properties and who are motivated to do some trading. This is simple exchanging. However, what happens if you desire someone else's building but he has no interest in anything you now own? Can a swap under these conditions still be arranged? Maybe. Now we may need a three-way swap to realize our objectives.

Here's how it could go:

"A" owns some property (basis: $100,000.00) that "C" is offering $150,000.00 for. "A" would be happy to sell and use the proceeds to buy a building owned by "B." But to do this, "A" will have a current tax on his $50,000.00 profit. To cut the tax man out of the deal, "A" has "C" buy "B's" building—and then "A" gives "C" his property in exchange for the building. The result—if it be an even exchange—no current tax.

While even trading does happen, in most cases there is some cash involved in the deal—paid by one or another to even things up. Tax laws call this type of cash payment which is added to an exchange, "boot." The person who receives the boot must pay taxes—but this tax is limited to the boot.

The one who renders boot, of course, pays no taxes.

While we highly recommend the consideration of making an exchange, we do feel a good tax expert (a CPA and/or tax attorney) should be consulted.

DEFERRED INSTALLMENT SALES

Here is a great method, at the option of the tax payer, to prorate gross profit over the period in which payments are received. The amount reported as gross profit in any year is determined by applying the gross profit percentage on a sale to the payments collected in that year. To use this special method, the seller must not receive payments or receive payments less than 30% of the selling price in the tax year of the sale. This technique can be put in practice whether or not there is an immediate conveyance of title. Installment reporting is an election. If no election is set forth, the entire gain is subject to tax. A big drawback to installment selling is that the seller must wait for his money over the term of the installment.

Here is a great technique to consider:

The installment seller takes the buyer's notes in the sale. The seller then gets a loan from his banker in the exact amount of sale and uses the buyer's notes as collateral. As the buyer pays off his obligation, the seller reduces his loan at his bank. The interest received on the notes should offset interest that will be required on the loan. And, now, the seller has full use of all of his money, without having to discount the notes.

135

CAPITAL GAINS

Another great tax advantage of real estate investing is the favorable capital gain tax rates (40% of the rate on your ordinary income). However, to qualify for these tax breaks you must operate within the rigid time limits set by law. The "holding period" is crucial. You will be taxed at capital gain rates only if you held the property within the prescribed time period: *One Year and one day* or more! The holding period starts the day after title passes or the day after delivery of possession, whichever happens first.

INCOME AVERAGING WITH CAPITAL GAINS

Capital gains render substantial tax savings because they allow you to be taxed at less than 50% the rate you would be required to pay on your ordinary income. Now, let's toss in Income Averaging to sweeten the pot! Tax law allows you to average your capital gains along with your ordinary income. Thus, you can treat any given one year of capital gains just as if you received them over a five-year period. Another potential super tax shelter!

To discover if you can apply income averaging, do this: multiply your average taxable income for the last four years by 120%. Now, deduct from your current year's taxable income (don't forget to include 40% of your long term capital gain). If the difference is over $3,000.00, you qualify for income averaging.

The more money you make, the bigger your tax savings can be. Let's look at this example:

Mr. Julian is married and has taxable ordinary income of $34,800.00. His average taxable income for the last four years is also $34,800.00. This year Mr. Julian has a long-term capital gain of $90,000.00 from the sale of real estate. He qualifies for income averaging. 120% of his average taxable income for the past four years is $41,760.00 ($34,800.00 x 120%). His current income, which includes 40% of his capital gain, is $70,800.00. The difference is $28,040.00, well above the $3,000.00 needed to qualify. By using this method, Mr. Julian will be saving a bundle at tax time.

Is income averaging always best? No, not always. If you employ income averaging, you will not be entitled to the maximum 50% tax rate on personal service income. Go over the advantages and disadvantages with your CPA or tax attorney.

Income averaging can be used effectively, whatever the reason for a big increase in your income. For the purposes of this manual, we emphasize real estate sales and capital gains. But it can also apply as a great tax-saver when you receive a big cash bonus or a substantial raise in your salary.

USING CAPITAL GAINS
WITH REAL ESTATE OPTIONS

For several years, sharp real estate investors have made nice profits in options. They cost only a small fraction of the property's purchase price. But if the property goes up in value during the time the investor holds the option (and this has been the usual case in the late 1970's and early 1980's), the option can be sold and essentially the same profit made as if the full purchase price had been paid. This is splendid use

137

of leverage, making big profits from small investments.

Example: You buy an option on a tract of land for $10,000.00. The present value is $100,000.00. The option lasts five years, and there is a 20% increase in the value during the time you hold your option. Now the land has a value of $120,000.00. Should you sell your option for $20,000.00, you have doubled your $10,000.00 investment in five years. You enjoy a 100% profit, even though the land only went up 20%.

Not only have you doubled your money in five years, but your $10,000.00 profit is taxed at the long-term capital gain rates. On the sale of an option, gain or loss is taxed at the same method as gain or loss on the property on which the option is being held. By holding your option for over the required holding period, your profit qualifies as a long-term capital gain.

TAX TIPS FOR LAND SALES

When a real estate investor buys land, the goal is usually to hang on to it till it soars in value, at which time it is sold at a profit. Since it is difficult to borrow money on land, sellers often have to take back a mortgage. With the exception of the down payment (if you're the seller, get all the cash you possible can up front), the balance is paid in installments. Unless you have tax savings on your mind, the seller could end up paying full tax in the year of the sale, even though he will not be receiving all of his money during the year. As I mentioned previously, if payments in the year of sale are less than 30% of the sale price, the tax man allows you to use installment reporting. In this matter, tax is only paid on the profit realized from payments received. This is a good way to go, but how many of us real estate investors will say "no" to a buyer who wants to make a down payment over 30%? Not very many. Using this technique we can receive more cash and still dodge another tax bullet.

Look at this example:

Fourteen years ago Mrs. Renwick bought 25 acres of land for only $12,500.00. The land has increased in value to $125,000.00. A builder now wants the land and offers Mrs. Renwick that much for the land with these terms:

(1) An immediate downpayment of $50,000.00
(2) The remaining $75,000.00 to be paid over a three year period.

Although Mrs. Renwick is looking at a big profit, she also is faced with paying capital gain tax on the full amount of the profit—$112,500.00. And she will only get $50,000.00 this year. Even though Mrs. Renwick can use income averaging, the tax is much higher than she wants to pay. She doesn't qualify for installment reporting since she will be receiving over 30% of the purchase price in the year of sale.

Taking a better approach, Mrs. Renwick then splits her 25 acres into two parcels of 15 acres and 10 acres. The builder buys one parcel he needs right away (the 10 acre one) for $50,000.00. Now, in a separate deal, Mrs. Renwick sells him the other 15 acre parcel for $75,000.00, with a small down-payment, taking back the 3-year mortgage for the rest of the purchase price. Using this tactic, Mrs. Renwick will pay a capital gain tax this year on only part of her profit. The second parcel land sale has qualified for an installment sale, thus she must pay a capital gain tax in each of the three following years only on the proportionate part of her profits. That's a tremendous savings in itself, but there is more; her split sale also lets her enjoy the first year cash benefits. By arranging two separate sales of her land, Mrs. Renwick collects over 40 percent of the combined sales price in the first year. That is a substantial increase over the 30 percent or less she would have received had it been limited to a single installment sale.

TAX-FREE RESIDENCE SALE BY HOME OWNERS

If you are 55 years old or over, you may avoid taxes on profits up to $100,000. on the sale of your home. To claim this special exclusion you must (1) elect to avoid tax; (2) be 55 or over prior to the sale date; and (3) have owned and occupied the house as your main residence for at least three of the five years prior to sale. Even if you cannot meet the three out of five year test, you could still qualify if you are 65 years old or over when you sell, and the home has been your main residence preceding a sale. This special exclusion can only be used one time in a person's life.

SYNDICATIONS

Syndications prove valuable when a job is too big for any individual to handle. While there is no basic difference between a syndicator and a regular real estate broker or salesman, he does have to be more sophisticated in putting together solid real estate investment packages.

If you wish to sell your own house or land, you are free to do so. However, if you want to do it for someone else, you need a license as a real estate salesman or broker. Also, if you intend to hire others to assist you in selling shares or units of real estate investments, it is up to you to make certain they are licensed to do this in the state where the sales will take place.

Real estate brokers and salesmen can sell properties, but unless they also have a securities license, they cannot sell securities. Only a small percentage of people hold both licenses, with the securities license. Make sure you are dealing with the correct agent if you do not hold the appropriate license yourself.

The forms of syndications are outlined on the following page:

The Corporation: While there are both pro and con tax considerations to forming your own corporation, limited liability, continuity of life and transfer of stock are among the chief attractions. Among the disadvantages are increased paperwork, tax reporting, recordkeeping, etc. . .

The Limited Partnership: This form can have two different types of partners: General partner(s) who look after the property and have unlimited liability or limited partners who have little to say regarding business decisions and no liability beyond their cash investments. Units of ownership can be transferred if desired and provisions can be made for continuity if required. It is attractive because it is simple, pays no taxes, allows tax shelters, profits and capital gains the same as if each partner were a single proprietor. It offers most of the advantages of the full corporate structure without many of the corporation's drawbacks. Using this kind of limited partnership, we have flexibility, limited liability for limited partners (their liability is only tied-in to their investments), guidance by a general partner, usually a developer who is on top of the situation, plus an opportunity to share in tax shelters in the same manner single investors can. The limited partnership is usually best for everyone except the mega-investor who desires the full corporate shield.

Since developers greatly differ on what special rights the general partner and the limited partners should hold, it is important to clearly spell out everyone's responsibilities when syndication and partnership papers are prepared. Some of the key points could be:

(A) What special rights should the general partner receive? Cash considerations? Ownership without investing? Profits only? Which one or combination of advantages, including others not listed here, should he receive?

(B) Under what considerations and circumstances should the limited partners be able to remove the general partner?

(C) What action is taken if a limited partner does not make a required payment?

(D) In what form should the financial report schedule be issued?

(E) Will the general partner be allowed to keep a commission on the sale of property if he is a licensed broker?

(F) Should the general partner be permitted to own units of the limited shares?

By having an attorney draw up the articles of the partnership in a concise fashion, many future headaches can be avoided. It is not only fair and square but also absolutely important that everyone involved in an investing project fully understand what is required of each member of the partnership.

THE TAX LAW, RAW LAND AND TIMBER

Those hunting for raw land real estate opportunities are often drawn to the advantages of land that has lots of standing timber. Timber can offer strong advantages of raw land that lies in the path of future development. It is now very difficult to find good buys on prime land that sits close to a growing city or town. Prices are usually at or near the top of the market. The better buys in the 1980's and beyond will be found farther removed from the current heavily populated areas. Good buying opportunities can be found in rural areas, but investments here are still no piece of cake. After you purchase raw land, you will have to sit back and wait for values to rise. In the meantime, expenses will be doing their number on you. Every year you will be paying interest on your mortgage plus property taxes.

Taxes and payments are what makes raw land with timber on it so attractive. The timber can offer you a nice return until you are ready to sell. Also, raw land with standing timber offers real tax advantages. You pay no taxes until the timber is cut. You can even receive capital gain treatment when the cutting does take place. And here's the kicker: you can even offset or completely deplete the capital cost of your timber investment against your sale proceeds.

First you must find the land. Don't fret; you should have no problem finding plenty of raw land in your area with standing timber. Look for undeveloped raw land. It is readily available and the cheapest kind. Just make certain there are roads adjoining your raw land investments. It is too risky to buy land that does not offer adjoining roads. Sure, you can bet that roads will eventually be built, but what if eventually is a long, long time. Don't take this gamble. Raw land with plenty of timber on it and adjoining roads is available across the nation. Hop in the auto next Sunday and take a relaxing drive into the country nearest the city or town you live in. You should enjoy the scenery, the fresh air, and you may also find a top-notch investment opportunity.

After you locate land, you should make notes on the kind

144

of timber there is on it. It is usually wise to hire an expert to list the kinds of timber and the values of same. To get an accurate estimate how much timber there is—and what it is worth—on any given parcel of raw land, a timber cruise is required. The Revenue service has an excellent guidebook (Form T Guide) for this timber cruise.

A nice tax break in the capital-gain treatment is available to timber investors. To take advantage of this tax shelter you can sell the timber outright, grant timber-cutting rights for a royalty or chop down the timber yourself.

Example:

Mr. Richmond has owned a parcel of raw land with standing timber for years. He originally paid $25,000.00 for this tract. By allocating $15,000.00 of the purchase price for the standing timber (consult your tax expert), Mr. Richmond is in a great position to shelter future profits. He can sell cutting rights for up to $15,000.00 and not be subjected to the sting of the taxman. At the same time, the land itself (if he has selected this parcel wisely) will be increasing in value, making way for a nice future profit at the time of sale.

MORE TAX SAVING TIPS

10% INVESTMENT CREDIT
FOR THE COST OF REHABILITATING
INDUSTRIAL OR COMMERCIAL BUILDINGS

The tax boys offer an excellent savings—a 10 percent investment credit for speculators who rehabilitate or renovate commercial or industrial properties. The kind of property that qualifies for this tax savings are buildings at least twenty years old. Such as: hotels, motels, retail stores, office buildings, factories, warehouses and wholesale stores—almost any type of building, with the exception of residential property.

The investment credit is available for those expenses that improve the property, increase its useful life and/or upgrade for new or present use. The credit is extended for improvements on either the interior or the exterior. It can cover many different types of improvements: painting, roofing, air-conditioning, heating, plumbing, wiring, etc. To be eligible for the full 10 percent credit, all improvements must have a useful life of at least seven years. New construction (such as add-ons, a new wing, etc.) do not qualify for this special tax credit.

However, it is my educated guess that the 1980's will bring even greater tax advantages, especially to investors who make improvements to buildings in the nation's leading cities. There is a strong movement, begun in the 1970's, that should be in full swing by the mid-1980's to rebuild and rehabilitate many core cities. Cities like San Diego, Oakland, Boston, St. Paul and Atlanta have elaborate renovation projects in pro-

146

cess. Dozens of other leading cities are planning to do likewise.

Even bigger tax advantages are now available to investors who rehabilitate historic buildings.

If the property you purchase and renovate has historic significance, you may be able to take advantage of a super tax shelter. Check with City Hall to make certain it is "Certified Historic Structure." If you can't get the information there, contact your state's Historic Preservation Officer. He also has the necessary papers you will need. If the site you are considering purchasing is not yet certified but you think it has a chance to qualify (it is estimated that over half a million buildings in America can qualify), the Historic Preservation Officer has forms that you can fill out in the hopes of obtaining certification.

Investors in a historic property have a choice of two special tax breaks:

(A) The Accelerated Depreciation Method. In using this method you can take depreciation deductions as if you were the original owner of the building. You can use 200 percent declining balance depreciation if you renovate for residential use (historic buildings can be residential, industrial or commercial) instead of the normal 125 percent declining balance used for most other types of buildings. If you make improvements for industrial or commercial use, you can use the 150 percent declining balance method (instead of straight-line only). You can also take rapid depreciation on BOTH the cost of the building and the rehab costs.

147

(B) Five-Year Writeoff. Using this method you can write off your rehabilitation costs over just five years—rather than the building's longer actual useful life. This can bring a huge tax savings!

Example:

Mr. Hays buys a rundown building for $50,000.00 ($40,000.00 for the building, $10,000.00 for the land). The Government certifies that it is an "historic structure" and approves his rehab plans. He then obtains $200,000.00 (financial institutions are usually most willing to finance renovation of an historic structure), and he rehabilitates the property and divides it into three rental units. Mr. Hays now has two choices:

(1) He can use the 200 percent declining balance depreciation to write off the entire $140,000.00 (building cost plus rehab expenses). Using this method, he will get an $11,200.00 deduction the first year.

—or—

(2) He can write off the $100,000.00 rehab cost over five years—getting $20,000.00 in deductions each year. Mr. Hays will also be able to take a $2,000.00 depreciation deduction on the building shell in year one, using the 125 percent declining balance.

With these kinds of big tax shelters, investors should be looking hard for potential historic opportunities.

A final word . . . .

Saving money can accomplish the same task as earning money. The money you save on taxes gives you more spendable income. Take every single tax deduction possible in all your business transactions. Since all accountants and attorneys are not equal, search long and hard till you find men or women who know their tax laws well. Seek out the best professional help available. When it comes to saving money on taxes, you need all the help you can get.

NOTES

APPENDIX A

Cash Flow

Cash flow is the amount of cash left over from gross receipts after all cash expenses. Cash expenses do not include depreciation.

For example, if we had an annual gross income (before expenses) of $12,000 and had actual operating expenses (including payments) of $10,000, there would be $2,000 left over. This 2,000 is what we are putting into our pockets before we include depreciation.

Cash flow = Gross income-Expenses (including payments)
$$CF = GI - E$$

APPENDIX B

Vacancy Factor

In figuring a vacancy factor, the lower the rate, the more in your pocket.

Every unit has an occupancy of 365 days. We prefer to use 365 days rather than 360. If we had 10 days vacancy—

$$\frac{10}{360} = 2.77\% \text{ while } \frac{10}{365} = 2.73\%$$

the vacancy rate would be a fraction of that 365 expressed first as a fraction and then as a decimal. For example, if our unit were vacant 36 days then—

$$\frac{36}{365} = 9.86\%$$

If our rent was $1,000 per year, then the expense of our vacancy expressed as dollars would be—

$$9.86\% \times \$1,000 \text{ or } \$98.60$$

Remember that it is common practice to deduct 10% vacancy factor as an expense. Anything you can prove to a buyer that is less than 10% is money in your pocket. See why you don't lose money if you move someone in for a few days free rent?

APPENDIX C

Property Tax Evaluation

When the assessor appraises your property, he breaks tax dollars into 3 parts:

(a) Land

(b) Improved property (buildings and structures and

(c) Personal property (furniture, carpets, etc.)

This tax can then be broken down into percentages of each. This is usually used to determine your basis and how much depreciation you can use.

The government does not permit the **land** to be depreciated because theoretically it doesn't wear out.

The **improved property** will wear out so you are permitted to defray the cost of that building over a period of time. (The shorter the time, the higher the depreciation figure.) If the assessor determines that 70% of your property is improved property, then certainly the IRS will recognize that as being a fair figure. (You can set up a larger percentage, but you may be challanged by IRS to justify the basis).

The **personal property** would be those furnishings which are not part of the structure. Furniture, carpets, appliances, etc. These don't have the longevity of the structures, so they can receive an "excellerated" depreciation (depreciated in a much shorter span). The average estimated life for carpets in an apartment for instance, can be 5 years.

APPENDIX D

Effect of Income on the Value of Property

Capitalization Method

$$\text{Value} = \frac{\text{Net Income}}{\text{Capitalization Rate}}$$

An investor is going to expect a greater return on his money if the risk is higher. His return on income property is based on income. The more that is subtracted in expenses from that income, the less the value of the property. The better your property looks on paper, the better price it should bring.

The **capitalization rate** is not a constant figure. It is the rate of return an investor wants for a particular property. If the post office were to sign a lease for 20 years, there would be little risk, therefore a small return would be expected. If this same amount were invested in an older slum building that would require greater maintenance and vacancy, a higher rate would be expected.

Your city has different risk levels depending on area, age of buildings, vacancy and many other factors. This capitalization rate could vary from 5% (the post office) to 25% (our slum building). By closely studying the want ads you should be able to determine what the current rates are - certainly any knowledgable realtor would know - give him a call. For this example, 8% will be used.

Step 1

gross income—total revenue received from all means

less expenses—management fees, utilities, taxes, insurance services, repairs, paint, etc.

Net Income

The **Net Income divided by** the **capitalization rate** gives us the **Value** of the property.

Value = Net income ÷ Capitalization rate

If the net income is 5600 annually and we use a capitalization rate of 8%

$$.08 \overline{\smash{)}\,5600.00} \quad 70,000$$

The value of the property by capitalization would be 70,000.

Gross Multiplier Method

There is another way of approximating property value from the gross income called the "gross multiplier" (either monthly or annually). Since this figure doesn't take expenses into consideration, it gives you only a "ball park" figure.

With an annual gross multiplier of 8 and a gross income of $12000, then the value would be $96,000.

(8 x 12,000 = 96.000)

APPENDIX E

Depreciation

Definition: The amount ascribed to charging off the depreciating value of an aging property. This property could be a building, it could be improvements, it could even include producing plants, trees or vines.

Formerly an investor could start depreciation anew with each property when he acquired it.* IRS has changed this rule. Your depreciation now is carried from step to step when exchanged. Depreciation that has been written off is also subtracted from subsequent future properties as they are acquired.

A couple of terms come into focus at this time:

Recapture refers to IRS expectations of recapturing all or a portion of depreciation when property is sold. This recapture, depending on the type of depreciation used, will be either ordinary income or capital gain.
Cross-over point is the point in real estate investment where depreciation is no longer sufficient to render the property a tax loss.

*Therefore it is wise for the investor, **especially the estate builder,** to take out as little depreciation as possible or only as needed. This insures him more tax shelter down the road when he will need it more. This is also a clue as to why some of your early properties might be sold rather than exchanged. Somewhere in this process it might be to the investor's advantage to start anew with depreciation.

In intricate situations like these a knowledgeable realtor or tax advisor is worth the cost.

There are three basic methods of computing depreciation:

1. straight line method

2. declining balance method and,

3. sum of the digits method.

Straight line method - An equal amount is deducted each year until the entire value of the building is charged off. For tax purposes, this amount is charged off as an expense to the business. To find the depreciation, you divide the cost of the depreciable improvements by the economic life. What determines the economic life is somewhat debatable. The shorter the life, the greater the depreciation. The estate planner is not looking for tax shelter initially - he should try to gauge this just sufficiently to avoid paying taxes on his property's income.

If we have a $100,00 building on a $33,000 lot, we can charge off that $100,000. If we elect a 40 year anticipated life for the building-

$$40 \overline{)\begin{array}{c} 2,500 \\ 100,000 \end{array}}$$

we would charge $2,500 annually as an expense.

Declining balance method - Different types of new or used assets are depreciated at various rates such as 125%, 150%, or 200% of the original cost. This is known as an **accelerated method of depreciation**. For an estate builder this is not recommended. The more we charge off now, the less we will have to charge off later when we have more money involved.

These depreciation rates are really a variation of the straight line rate. If straight line rate is 2% (100,000 for 50 years), a 200% declining balance would be just double that - or 4%.

We would depreciate 100,000 4% the first year -

100,000 x .04 4,000
100,000 - 4,000 96,000

The second year we would depreciate -

96,000 x .04 3,840
96,000 - 3,840 92,160

The third year we would depreciate 92,160.

We would annually be depreciating from a **declining balance**.

Sum of the digits method - This is an accelerated method of depreciation available only for new assets (not buildings). This is based on the expected life (or what the IRS will allow). We will depreciate something with an expected life of 5 years for example.

Add up the aggregate numbers from 1 to 5.

1 + 2 + 3 + 4 + 5 = 15

Now go backwards and take 5/15 of its value as depreciation the first year, 4/15's the second year, and so on until the last year when you take 1/15. If we were depreciating 10,000 worth of furniture the first year we could deduct

$$(5/15 = 1/3)$$
$$1/3 \times 10{,}000 = \$3{,}333.33$$

The second year we could deduct-

$$4/15 = 2.666$$
$$2.666\% \times 10{,}000 = 2666.70$$

The third year we could deduct-

$$3/15 = 1/5$$
$$1/5 \times 10{,}000 = 2{,}000.00$$

The fourth year-

$$2/15 = .1333$$
$$1.333\% \times 10{,}000 = 1333.33$$

The fifth year-
$$1/15 = 6.666\%$$
$$6.66 \times 10{,}000 = 666.67$$
Total 10,000

When **accelerated depreciation** is used, the IRS is expecting **recapture** as **ordinary income,** not capital gains.

$$10\% \ .10 \times 100,000 = 10,000$$

(amount of depreciation to be taken on personal property)
If taken 5 years using sum of digits method

$$1 + 2 + 3 + 4 + 5 = 15$$
$$5 \times 10,000 - 1/3 \times 10\ 000 = 3,333.333$$

(1st year depreciation)

2nd year not as much

$$4/15 \times 10,000 = 2,666.67$$

Straight line annual depreciation	2,000
Sum of Digits on personal property	+ 3,333.33
Total depreciation to be included	(5,333.33)

as annual expense for tax purposes

For simplication on our example, we have disregarded the item on **interest.** It is a paper expense. In the early years of a Trust Deed almost all of the payment is going to interest. That portion going to principal (your equity) is negligible. To continue our over simplification, we are going to lean a little bit and say that all the payment is going to interest. Therefore all our payments are expense (but paper expense).

Income	Expense	cash expenses
12,000	4,000	interest
	+7,000	
12,000	−11,000	= (1,000 cash flow)
	+5,333.33	
12,000		
−16,333.33	16,333.333	Total expenses for
		tax purposes
(4,333.33	loss-tax shelter	

Sample Property

In order to give an example of many of these terms, we are going to buy a piece of property.

100,000	purchase price
30,000	down payment
12,000	gross annual income
4,000	annual expenses (not including interest or depreciation)
1,000	taxes (land 200, improvements 700, personal 100)
7,000	total annual payments
8%	capitalization rate (8 gross multiplier)
33	total days of vacancy

$$\text{Value} = \frac{\text{Net Income}}{\text{Capitalization rate}} = \$8,000$$

$$\text{Value} = \frac{\text{Net Income}}{\text{Capitalization rate}} \quad \frac{-\ \$8,000}{.08} = \$100,000$$

(Value by Capitalization Method)

Value Gross multiplier x gross income
8 x 12,000 = $96,000
(Value by gross multiplier method)

$$\text{Vacancy factor} \quad \frac{33}{365} = .09 \text{ or } 9\%$$

Vacancy factor expressed as dollar value

$9\% = .09 \times \$12,000 = \$1,080$

Gross Income minus $(-)$ cash expenses $-$ payments $=$ cash flow
$12,000 - (4,000 - 7,000) = 1,000$
Property tax breakdown
  Taxes 1,000
  Improvements 700

$$\begin{array}{r} .70 \\ 1,000 \overline{)\,700.00} \end{array} = 70\%$$

$$\begin{array}{r} .10 \\ 1,000 \overline{)\,700.00} \end{array} = 10\%$$

Personal property
70% .70 x 100,000 70,000
(amount of depreciation to be taken on building)

Straight Line Method 35 years
70,000 35 = $2,000 per year depreciation on building

163

APPENDIX G

Sequence of Foreclosure

1. **Delinquency** - there is nothing to say how delinquent an account might be before foreclosure proceedings can be started. Actually, agreements are written into some contracts whereby the trust deed holder considers the owner delinquent if he doesn't keep the property up to standard. Most trust deed holders wait until 2½ - 4 months before filing.

2. **Notice of default** - This shows the intent of the trust deed holder. It gives the occupant a period of 90 days to catch the account up to date. If the occupant has a sizeable equity in the property, he is motivated to sell and lots of people know it. The owner can also borrow money to pay the delinquent amount (and sometimes borrow more). For this amount, the owner can sign a note promising to pay a given amount at monthly intervals - the new lender than records this as a new trust deed. Because the former existing trust deed holds priority over this, the new trust deed is called a junior lien. There can be as many junior trust deeds as there are people who will lend money. Toward the end of the 90 day period the delinquent is progressively more motivated to sell, because the situation becomes more acute after that 90th day.

3. **Twenty-one day notice** After the 90 day period has elapsed, the debtor is obliged to pay off the entire outstanding amount owed (plus penalties). This means that he must find someone to refinance the whole amount or that he must sell out without 21 days.

A popular approach by speculators is to have the delinquent sign off all rights to his property. This can be done through the vehicle of a **quit claim deed.** In order to get him to do this, you offer the delinquent cash for his signature. It is then up to you to satisfy the trust deed holder. (In this 21 day period, the trust deed holder is apt to let the account come back to current status.) Perhaps you can talk him into rescinding the whole foreclosure. If not, then you will have to pay the entire balance.

4. If the trust deed holder stands firm for the entire amount owing, he will set up a date and place for a **Trustee Sale.** By law, this must be advertised weekly in a paper of major circulation for a period of 3 weeks preceding the sale. (Obviously, this is started 3 weeks prior to the end of the 90 day period). Sometimes the auctions are held within the lending institution, sometimes on the steps of the county courthouse. The auction is begun at the figure owed the party calling for the sale and the action proceeds from that figure.

APPENDIX H

Sample Properties

Here are some examples of actual properties, sales and transactions that took place in Southern California within a four week period in July and August, 1978. Opportunities like this are always available—it only takes a little diligence and digging on your part to seek them out.

Sample Property #1

July 3, 1978

A four bedroom house in Southeast San Diego was probably worth $45,000 with an existing $28,000 balance on the First Trust Deed.

The Second Trust Deed was being foreclosed upon at $3,500. There was only one qualified (with cash or cashier's checks) bidder who bid $1 over the Trust Deed original bid.

$$\begin{array}{r} \$28,000 \\ +\ \ 3,500 \\ \hline \$31,500 \end{array}$$

$$\begin{array}{r} \$45,000 \\ -\ 31,500 \\ \hline \$14,500 \end{array}$$

$$\$14,500 \div \$3,501 = 400\ \% \text{ profit}$$

July 25, 1978

The San Diego County Administrator held an auction of five properties. Several sold under the appraised value. Here are two illustrations:

Sample Property #2

One Vista property was appraised at $47,800 and was sold at $45,000. My feeling is that with only a little gardening and a little cosmetizing, this home would be worth about $52,000. This is right next to freeways and shopping centers in a very popular area. It could sell or rent easily.

Sample Property #3

A Rancho Bernardo home was appraised at $70,000, which is a low appraisal. This was auctioned at $70,500. Needing only some minor gardening and painting, this residence would easily bring $80,000 on the market. Rancho Bernardo is extremely popular, and there are few properties that bring less than $79,000—and those are smaller and with fewer bathrooms.

July 24, 1978

Under the flagpole at the La Jolla Post Office, two La Jolla glamour properties were auctioned under two different trustee sales (same trustor and trustee).

Sample Property #4

This house was appraised at $125,000. The total trust Deed outstanding balances totaled $88,000. The $25,000 Second Trust Deed being foreclosed upon was purchased at $36,000. This home needed painting, carpeting and drapes. If we assume $10,000 for upgrading and back taxes:

$$\$1,000 \ \& \ \$36,000 = \$46,000 \text{ cash investment}$$
$$\$125,000 - \$88,000 = \$37,000 \text{ equity}$$
$$\$37,000 \div \$46,000 = 80\% \text{ profit}$$

Sample Property #5

The other property was a large glamour executive home for entertaining with a fantastic view of La Jolla Shore. It was surrounded by homes valued at hundreds of thousands of dollars.

It was the consensus of many that the property was worth $200,000. (In fact, it was in escrow at the time for $197,000.) It finally sold for what totaled $188,000. Somehow, this represents 6% under the market! Although this auction was spectacular (about 50 present with about 7 bidders) and still bought at a dollar price bargain, percentagewise it would not have been as good an investment as some others.

Sample Property #6

August 3, 1978

In December, 1976, a man paid $125,000 for a 2,000 + square foot contemporary home on a site with a view in San Diego County. The property was on a slight hill covering 2½ acres, completely enclosed with cyclone fence, horse corrals and about ½ acre in fruit trees. This is a prestigious neighborhood, with valuable horse ranches and classic old home.

Twenty months later at a trustee sale, this property was sold for:

$96,000	on the 1st TD
$25,000	on the 2nd TD
$ 2,000	on delinquent taxes
$123,000	

Property in San Diego County in 1977 on the average appreciated 33%. In the choice areas (such as this), the average was more. This property was easily worth:

$175,000
-123,000
‾‾‾‾‾‾‾‾‾‾
$52,000   equity

The Second Trust Deed was foreclosed upon, and the penalties and costs brought the opening bid to approximately $34,000 and eventually sold for $35,000.

$52,000 ÷ 35,000 = 148.5% (if sold at $175,000)

Sample Property #7

August 9, 1978

A representative of the government (FNMA) held a trustee sale and no qualified bidders showed up. The property went back to the government for $44,670. Although run down, this place, with cosmetizing, would be a classy property with Pt. Loma, Coronado and San Diego Harbor view. It is in an area of mixed cultures.

It should be worth over $50,000—no real investment bargain. It will be completely refurbished by the government and sold as an FHA foreclosure and picked up for very little down—that could be a good investment if one would live there for a while and later sell it.

Sample Property #8

August 11, 1978

There was a sheriff's sale of 160 acres near Palomar Observatory. Eighty acres had been purchased for $80,000 and the other eighty for only about $12,000. This property, difficult to appraise, had to be worth $125,000.

Against this man was a judgment for $10,252 plus about $410 in expenses. This property was bid on at the judgment price and penalty only —there were no other bidders—not even any other observers:

$$\$125,000 \div \$10,660 = 1,172\% \text{ profit}$$

Summary of Sample Properties

After working TRUSTEE sales, PROBATE sales and SHERIFF sales full time for only a total of three weeks, it is obvious that there are bargains out there . Although one can spend vast amounts of time researching these properties, the bargains are there—and some outright steals. The higher cost properties aren't necessarily the best bargains. The better bargains seem to be away from the metro areas, with the exception of the submarginal areas. As previously suggested, suburban property listed by legal description only and posted only in the sheriff's office are often completely overlooked.

NOTES

173

GLOSSARY

APPRECIATION - the increase in property value. (3)

APARTMENTS - as a good investment (10)

BOOT - any cash, securities or property of a different type received in a "like kind" exchange. (7)

BARGAINS - on forecolsures (8)

    due to divorce (8)

    - estate sales (9)

    - FHA and VA resales (9)

CAPITALIZATION, rate of - the formula of Net Annual In come divided by the Rate of Yield equals Estimated Value. (6)

CAPITAL GAIN - cash profit gained in a transaction. (7)

COUNTY RECORDER'S OFFICE - as information source (9)

CONVERSION - of older houses, etc. (10)

CONDOMINIUMS - conversion to (10)

DEED OF TRUST - (8)

DEFAULT, notice of - a recorded notice meaning that you are behind in loan payments. (8-9)

DEPRECIATION - the decrease in property value. (3)

DEFERRED TAX - resulting from trade or exchange (7)

EQUITY - the appraised money value of a property above and beyond any liens against it. (3)

FORECLOSURE - the legal procedure where property is sold through court ordered auction because of default. (4, 8, 9)

GRAFTING - buying two similar properties and putting them together to boost your equity. (6)

INFLATION - and buying power (2)

    - how to minimize effects of (6, 7)

    - and appreciation (3)

IRS (INTERNAL REVENUE SERVICE)
- and depreciation (3)
- "like kind" definition (7)
- tax advantages for trade or exchange (7)
- Section 1031 (7)

INCOME PROPERTY
- kinds of returns (5)
- calculating values (6)
- rents (6)
-residential (9)

LAND CONTRACT - a method where the seller keeps the title in his name and the buyer makes payments as contracted in the sellers name. (4)

LEASE OPTION - leasing a property with the option of buying. (4)

LEVERAGE - Using other peoples money with as little of your own as possible to buy property. (3)

"LIKE KIND" - IRS definition (7)

LIMITED PARTNERSHIP - a partnership made up of General and Limited partners who have all invested in the same property. (12)

MONEY - how to find for investment (4)

NEGATIVE CASH FLOW - renting a property for less than the payment. (4)

"NEW STARTER" - grafting (3,6)
- FHA and VA resales (9)

OTHER PEOPLE'S MONEY (OPM) - corporate use of (3)
- financing your wealth with (4)
- using (5)

PROPERTY - income, values (5)
- why values rising (6)

REALTORS - finding right one (11)

SECOND DEED OF TRUST - same as second mortgage (4)

SECOND MORTGAGE - (second deed of trust) a way to get a loan secured by property you own.

SYNDICATION - the joining of two or more people for investment purposes. (Chpt. 12)

TAX DEFERRED INCOME - income that you do not have to pay taxes on immediately. (7)

TAX RATES (10)

TAX SHELTER - buying and selling procedures that protect your money from taxation. (3)

TAX SHELTER, ADVANTAGES - for trade or exchange (7)

TRADE OR EXCHANGE - as tax shelter (7)
 - when cash is involved (10)

BIBLIOGRAPHY

Freshman, Samuel K.
  Principles of Real Estate Syndication
  Parker & Son, Los Angeles, CA

Haroldson, Mark O.
  How to Wake up the Financial Genius Inside You.
  Marko Enterprises, Salt Lake City, Utah

Nickerson, William
  How I turned $1,000 into a Million in Real Estate-in my
  spare time. Simon & Schuster, New York, NY

McClean, L.
  McClean's Property Pyramid
  Nides Cini Publications, Los Angeles, CA

McMichael, Stanley L.
  How to Make Money in Real Estate
  Wilshire Book Company, North Hollywood, CA

Nielson, Jens & Jackie
  How to Save or Make Thousands when you buy or sell
  your house. Dolphin Books, Doubleday & Co. Inc.,
  Garden City, NY

Allen, Robert G.
  Nothing Down
  Simon and Schuster, New York, NY

Bockl, George
  How to Use Leverage to Make Money in Local Real Estate
  Prentice Hall, Englewood Cliffs, NJ

Gillig, Harry
Real Estate Money-Matters - How to Mine the Hidden
Gold in Local Real Estate, Institute for Business Planning,
Inc., Englewood Cliffs, NJ

Glubetich, Dave
The Monopoly Game - the "How To" book of making big
money with rental homes, Impact Publishing Company,
Pleasant Hill, CA

Greenberg, Calvin L.
Profit Opportunities in Real Estate Investments
Prentice Hall, Englewood Cliffs, NJ

Hale, Bruce M.
Your Cash Profits - An Easy Guide to Real Estate and Law
National Institute of Financial Planning, Inc., Salt Lake
City, UT

Hicks, Tyler G.
How to Make One Million Dollars in Real Estate in Three
Years Starting with No Cash, Prentice Hall, Englewood
Cliffs, NJ

Lowry, Albert J.
How You Can Become Financially Independent by Investing in Real Estate, Simon and Schuster, New York, NY

NOTES